Priscilla Hauser's
PAINTED
FURNITURE

Priscilla Hauser

Sterling Publishing Co., Inc.
New York

PROLIFIC IMPRESSIONS PRODUCTION STAFF:

Editor in Chief: Mickey Baskett
Copy Editor: Phyllis Mueller
Graphics: Dianne Miller, Karen Turpin
Photography: Joel Tressler
Administration: Jim Baskett

Every effort has been made to insure that the information presented is accurate. Since we have no control over physical conditions, individual skills, or chosen tools and products, the publisher disclaims any liability for injuries, losses, untoward results, or any other damages which may result from the use of the information in this book. Thoroughly read the instructions for all products used to complete the projects in this book, paying particular attention to all cautions and warnings shown for that product to ensure their proper and safe use.

Library of Congress Cataloging-in-Publication Data Available

10 9 8 7 6 5 4 3 2 1

Published by Sterling Publishing Co., Inc.
387 Park Avenue South, New York, N.Y. 10016

© 2003 by Prolific Impressions, Inc.

Produced by Prolific Impressions, Inc.
160 South Candler St., Decatur, GA 30030

Distributed in Canada by Sterling Publishing
c/o Canadian Manda Group, One Atlantic Avenue, Suite 105
Toronto, Ontario, Canada M6K 3E7
Distributed in Great Britain by Chrysalis Books
64 Brewery Road, London N7 9NT, England
Distributed in Australia by Capricorn Link (Australia) Pty. Ltd.
P.O. Box 704, Windsor, NSW 2756 Australia

Printed in China
All rights reserved
Sterling ISBN 1-4027-0339-2

ACKNOWLEDGEMENTS

• This book could never have become a reality without my painting team — **Barbara Sondrup, Rosanne Mapp,** and **Sonja Claes.** They deserve tremendous credit for their hours of sanding, basecoating, and painting.

• I thank my editor, **Mickey Baskett,** for creative ideas and inspiration.

• Credit for the completion of this book is due in large part to my editorial and backup staff — **Naomi Meeks, Sue Sensintaffar, Judy Kimball,** and **Connie Deen.** The words "thank you" are inadequate, but they are heartfelt.

• I would like to thank the following manufacturers for their generous donation of painting supplies and for their support of my work.
Plaid Enterprises, Inc., www.plaidonline.com., for FolkArt® Acrylic Artist Pigments and Acrylic Colors; Painting Mediums; Crackling Medium; and Artist Lacquers.
Loew-Cornell, Inc., www.loew-cornell.com, for high-quality artist brushes.
Masterson, www.mastersonart.com, for the Sta-Wet Palette.

About Priscilla Hauser

She has been called "first lady of decorative painting" because of her early involvement in the teaching of the craft and her key role in organizing the first meeting of the National Society of Tole and Decorative Painters on October 22, 1972. Since that first meeting, attended by Priscilla Hauser and 21 others, the organization has thrived, and so has Priscilla.

From her beginning efforts as a tole painter in the early 1960s, when she took classes at a YMCA in Raytown, Missouri, Priscilla Hauser has become a world-renowned teacher and author and the decorative painting industry's ambassador to the world. She has traveled to teach in England, Canada, Japan, Argentina, and The Netherlands and has instructed extensively throughout the United States and at her Studio by the Sea in Panama City Beach, Florida. Besides teaching, Priscilla has illustrated her techniques through books,

magazine articles, videos, and television. The results of her teaching program have led to an accreditation program for teachers.

Priscilla says to everyone, "I can teach you to paint. Come paint with me in my beautiful Studio by the Sea! You will learn the basics: brush strokes, double-loading, blending, and proper preparation of surfaces. You'll even learn some pen-and-ink techniques and some fabric painting." Priscilla's seminars are extremely valuable to beginners as well as more advanced painters. Her methods teach the newcomer and strengthen the experienced. The seminars last five-and-a-half days and, after studying for 100 hours, you can become accredited with the Priscilla Hauser Program.

To receive seminar details, send for Priscilla Hauser's Seminar Brochure and Schedule, P.O. Box 521013, Tulsa, OK 75152-1013.

CONTENTS

THE PROJECTS
page 29

7

Introduction

Every room in your home needs at least one piece of painted furniture. A marvelous painted piece can set the scene for the spirit of the whole room – it's what decorators call a "conversation piece."

If the pieces in this book could talk, what interesting stories they could tell! All were found in bad condition. With a little time, elbow grease, and determination, each has become a little masterpiece. Family heirlooms that need restoring or the tattered, worn piece spotted at a garage sale can be fabulous with just a little tender loving care.

The projects in this book are easy, and the instructions are detailed and complete. Read and study them carefully. Then I dare you to use your own imagination and color ideas.

I hope this book can help you discover how much fun it is to do it yourself, and that you enjoy it so much that you'll want to do more and more in the way of furniture painting.

PREPARING YOUR PROJECT

The amount of preparation you do depends on the condition of the piece. For the projects in this book, I used mostly older pieces I found at flea markets. It is fun to find the perfect piece and transform it from a throwaway to a treasure. New, unfinished wood pieces also can be used for painting the designs in this book.

I've included my tips for using both old and new pieces. Different types of background treatments require different preparations. Individual project instructions will tell you what to do to achieve a particular effect.

Old Pieces

If you are fortunate enough to find pieces that have already been painted and you like the color, it saves a tremendous amount of time. Often, I love the finish that is on an old piece I've purchased to decorate. If the paint is in good condition, cleaning the piece with soap and water and allowing it to dry completely may be all that's needed.

Here's how to clean an old piece:

To remove dirt, dust, cobwebs, or grease, use a cleaner that does not leave a gritty residue. Effective cleaners include **mild dishwashing detergent** and **bubble bath**. Mix the cleaner with water and wash the furniture with a cellulose sponge. Rinse and wipe dry with soft cloth rags. Let dry completely.

If the paint is chipped or flaking, but you want to keep the paint color and the old, distressed look, you will need to clean it and remove some of the chipped paint so your new painting won't flake away.

To prepare the original finish of an old piece for decoration:
1. Sand away any loose paint.
2. Wipe with a tack cloth.
3. Wipe with a liquid sanding preparation. Let dry thoroughly.
4. Transfer the design and proceed with painting.

If the paint cannot be rescued, if you don't like the color, or you don't want an aged look, a freshly painted basecoat may be required. The basecoat is the paint you apply to the

Sanding the existing finish on a blue-painted piece to remove loose and flaking paint.

surface before the design is transferred. Before you start, be sure the paint you apply is compatible with the type of paint you will use to do the decorative painting. If you are not sure, take a sample of your paint to a good paint store and ask them what type of paint you need for your basecoat.

Here's how to apply a new basecoat:
1. Clean the surface.
2. Using medium grade sandpaper, sand the surface thoroughly.
3. Wipe with a tack cloth.

4. Apply a coat of stain blocker or gesso. Allow to dry thoroughly and sand again. Wipe with a tack cloth.

5. Apply several coats of paint in your desired color, sanding between coats.

New Unfinished Wood Pieces

A painted basecoat provides the background for decorative painting. Generally, I don't seal raw wood before basecoating with acrylic paint because paint adheres better to unsealed wood. However, if there are knotholes or the wood is green, I apply a light coat of matte acrylic varnish to seal the flaws before applying paint.

Here's how to prepare a new piece for painting:

1. Sand piece with medium, then fine grade sandpaper. Wipe with a tack cloth.

2. Apply a light coat of varnish to seal any knotholes or green wood. Let dry.

3. If the sealer has raised the grain of the wood, sand lightly with fine sandpaper and wipe with a tack cloth.

Here's how to basecoat a new piece:

1. With a small roller, a foam brush, or a synthetic bristle brush, apply a generous amount of paint. You can use acrylic craft paint to basecoat the piece if the piece isn't too large. If you have a larger piece of furniture, a less expensive option for paint is to purchase paint in a larger container. You may be able to find "basecoating" paints at a craft store – OR you may purchase a small amount (a pint or quart) of latex satin-finish wall paint from a hardware store. Let dry.

2. Rub with a piece of a brown paper bag with no printing on it to smooth the painted wood.

3. Apply a second coat of the base color if needed for complete coverage. Let dry.

4. Use a piece of a brown paper bag to smooth the surface again. Sometimes a third coat of paint is necessary for full coverage.

Distressing Painted Pieces

Distressed finishes add the character imparted by use and age. You can create a simple distressed finish by scraping or sanding a painted piece to remove some of the paint, exposing layers of color (if there's more than one color of paint on the piece), and allowing some of the wood to show. This can be done with an old painted piece or a new piece you have just painted. The best places to sand are those areas where age would be most apparent, such as edges and handles.

You can create a timeworn look on a new piece as a background for a painted design.

Here's how to create a distressed look on a new piece:

1. Sand the piece and wipe with a tack cloth.

2. Apply two coats of ivory white (or other color) acrylic paint, using a 1" flat synthetic brush or a sponge brush. Allow the paint to dry between each coat.

3. When dry, sand the edges of the piece and here-and-there on the surface to give the item a worn look.

Lightly sanding a basecoated chair to give a distressed look.

SANDING TIPS

- Sand more on the edges of the piece – concentrating your efforts in places where wear would normally occur over time – and less on flat areas for a more natural appearance.

- Don't use a sanding block or an electric sander – you want an uneven look. Holding the sandpaper in your hand is best and allows you more control.

- Use medium or medium-fine grit sandpaper to remove more paint, fine grit sandpaper to remove less.

- It's best to begin slowly and err on the side of removing too little paint rather than too much. You can always sand again to remove more. Stop when the result pleases you.

BASIC PAINTING SUPPLIES

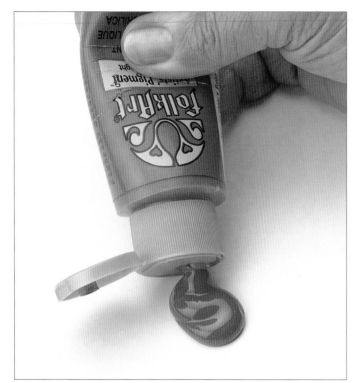

Acrylic paint is squeezed onto the palette.

Mix glazing medium with paint to make a glazing and antiquing mixture.

Paints

The projects in this book were painted with **artist pigment acrylics**. These rich, creamy, opaque paints come in squeeze bottles and are available at art supply and craft stores. They are a very high-quality paint for artists – and are packaged in a squeeze bottle rather than a tube. They have true pigment color names, just like oil paints. Their pigment is brilliant, and you can blend them and move them much in the same way as oil paints by using painting mediums.

Pre-mixed **acrylic craft paints** are available in hundreds of colors. These are not true pigment colors, but blended colors. They have the same consistency as artist pigment acrylics and can be used for decorative painting the same way as artist pigment acrylics. In this book, I use them to undercoat designs and for basecoating. If you choose paints from the same manufacturer, you can be sure they will be compatible with one another.

Mediums

Mediums are liquids or gels that are mixed with paint for achieving specific effects. They are sold along with acrylic paints. You will need floating medium and blending medium for each and every painting project.

Floating medium is used to thin the paint so that it can be used for floating a color. The brush is filled with the floating medium, then a corner of the brush is filled with color. After the brush is blended on the palette, the color is brushed along the edge of a design element to create shading or highlighting.

Blending medium is used to keep paint wet and moving. The medium is painted on the surface in the area of the design where you're painting, and the design is painted immediately while the blending medium is still wet.

Glazing medium is mixed with paint on a palette or in a small container to create a transparent glaze that can be used for antiquing or to create textured effects. This medium can also be used as a substitute for floating medium if you can not find floating medium. It works to thin the paint to an almost transparent glaze.

Palette

You will need a palette for all your painting projects. I like to use a "stay-wet" type palette. Some people prefer a wax-coated or dry palette for acrylics; however, I prefer a palette that stays wet since acrylics dry so quickly. Palettes can be found where decorative painting supplies are sold. A wet palette consists of a plastic tray that holds a wet sponge and special paper. To use this type of palette:

1. Soak the sponge in water until saturated. Do not wring out, but place the very wet sponge into tray.

2. Soak the paper that comes with the palette in water for 12-24 hours. Place the paper on top of the very wet sponge.

3. Wipe the surface of the paper with a soft, absorbent rag to remove the excess water.

4. Squeeze paint on the palette. When paints are placed on top of a properly prepared wet palette, they will stay wet for a long time.

Brushes

There are many different types of brushes, and different-shaped brushes do different things. You will need the four types of brushes in various sizes to do your decorative painting. The individual project instructions list the sizes of brushes needed for that particular project.

FLAT BRUSHES

Flat brushes are designed for brush strokes and blending. These brushes do most of the painting of the designs.

ROUND BRUSHES

Round brushes are used primarily for stroking – we seldom blend with them. They can also be used for some detail work.

FILBERT BRUSHES

Filbert brushes are a cross between a flat and a round brush. They are generally used for stroking, but can also be used for blending.

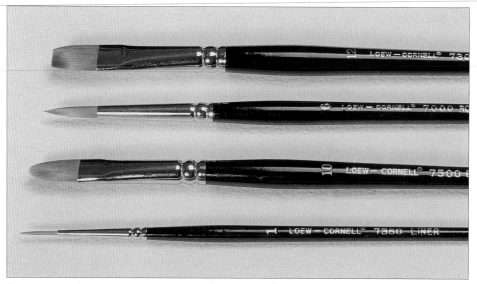

Brush types, **pictured top to bottom**: Flat, round, filbert, liner.

LINER BRUSHES

Liner brushes are very thin round brushes that come to a wonderful point. Good liner brushes are needed for fine line work.

When it comes to brushes, please purchase the very best that money can buy. They are your tools – the things you paint with. Occasionally, a student says, "Priscilla, I don't want to buy a good brush until I know I can paint." I always tell my students they won't be able to paint if they don't begin with a good brush. You get what you pay for.

Brush strokes are the basis of my decorative painting technique. This book includes excellent brush stroke worksheets for practicing. To use them, lay a sheet of acetate or tracing paper over the top of the worksheet, choose a brush large enough to make the same size strokes as shown on the worksheet, and practice hundreds of strokes on top of mine. (If a hundred sounds like a lot, get over it! You will find that painting a hundred strokes happens very quickly.)

BRUSH CARE

It's important to clean your brushes properly and keep them in excellent condition. To thoroughly clean them:

1. Gently flip-flop each brush back and forth in water until all the paint is removed, rinsing them thoroughly. Never slam brushes into a container and stir them. **(photo 1)**
2. Work brush cleaner through the hairs of the brush in a small dish **(photo 2)** and wipe the brush on a soft, absorbent rag. Continue cleaning until there is no trace of color on the rag.
3. Shape the brush with your fingers and store it so nothing can distort the shape of the hairs. Rinse the brush in water before using again.

Photo 1

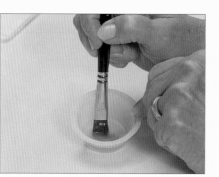

Photo 2

Other Paint Applicators

- **Sponge brushes** can be used for basecoating and for applying varnish. They are inexpensive and easy to use. I keep dozens of these brushes on hand.
  Stencil brushes can be used to pounce or dab paint on surfaces.

- **Sponge-on-a-stick applicators** are great for painting circular design motifs. They have thin round pieces of foam that are glued to the end of a dowel. The *Dragonfly Planter* project instructions has photos on page 107 showing a dragonfly being painted with one of these sponge applicators.

Basic Supplies for All Projects

These are the basic supplies that are needed for each project. They are not listed in the individual project instructions; you will, however, need to gather most of them for each and every project.

Sandpaper - I use sandpaper for smoothing unfinished and finished wood surfaces and for creating a distressed, aged look on painted surfaces. Sandpaper comes in various grades from very fine to very coarse. It's good to keep a supply on hand.

Tack Rag - A tack rag or tack cloth is a piece of cheesecloth or other soft cloth that has been treated with a mixture of varnish and linseed oil. It is very sticky. Use it for wiping a freshly sanded surface to remove all dust particles. When not in use, store the tack rag in a tightly sealed jar.

Brown Paper Bags - I use pieces of brown paper bags with no printing on them to smooth surfaces after basecoating and between coats of varnish.

Tracing Paper - I like to use a very thin, transparent tracing paper for tracing designs. I use a **pencil** for tracing.

Chalk, White and Colored - I use chalk for transferring the traced design to the prepared painting surface. Chalk will easily wipe away and not show through the paint. This is why I prefer it to graphite paper. Do not buy the dustless kind of chalk.

Transfer or Graphite Paper - Occasionally, I use white or gray graphite paper to transfer my design. However, I try to avoid using it because the lines may show through the paint. It can also make smudges on the background that are not easily removed.

Stylus - Use a stylus tool for transferring your traced design to the prepared surface. A pencil or a ballpoint pen that no longer writes also may be used.

Palette Knife - Use a palette knife for mixing and moving paint on your palette or mixing surface. I prefer a straight-blade palette knife made of flexible steel.

100% Cotton Rags - Use only 100% cotton rags for wiping your brush. *Try the knuckle test: For 15 seconds, rub your knuckles on the rag that you wipe your brush on. If your knuckles bleed, think of what that rag is doing to the hairs of your brush!* You could also use soft, absorbent **paper towels** for wiping brushes.

Water Basin: Use a water basin or other container filled with water for rinsing brushes.

Varnish: See "Finishing Your Piece" for details.

Basic Information

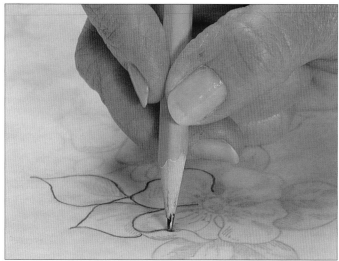
Photo 1

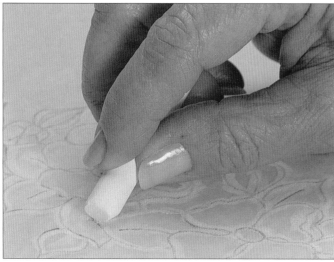
Photo 2

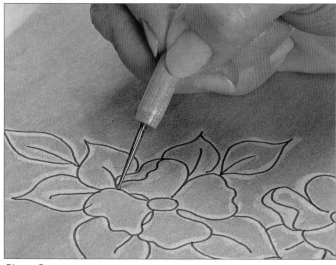
Photo 3

Transferring Patterns

TRANSFERRING A DESIGN WITH CHALK

1. Neatly trace the pattern of the design onto tracing paper. You may use a pencil or a pen. It is not necessary to trace shading lines or curlicues. (**photo 1**)
2. Turn over the traced design. Firmly go over the traced lines on the back with chalk. (**photo 2**) Do not scribble all over the tracing with the chalk.
3. Shake off the excess chalk dust, being careful not to inhale the particles.
4. Position the design on the prepared surface, chalk side down. Using a stylus, go over the lines. (**photo 3**) Don't press so hard that you make indentations in the surface. The chalk will be transferred to your surface. Chalk is easily removed and it dissolves as you paint over it.

TRANSFERRING A DESIGN WITH GRAPHITE

This is done the same way as the chalk technique, but instead of tracing over the back of the pattern with chalk, I trace over the back of the pattern with a #2 graphite pencil. I do this when I'm transferring to a very light surface where chalk lines may not show or when the chalk lines won't be precise enough, such as for inking a design. Graphite lines can be easily erased from a surface.

TRANSFERRING A DESIGN WITH TRANSFER PAPER

It is fine to transfer designs to a surface with white or gray transfer paper; however, this is my least favorite way to transfer a design because transfer paper tends to smudge. Here's how to use transfer paper:

1. Trace the pattern neatly and carefully from the book on tracing paper, using a pencil or fine point marker. Enlarge or reduce the pattern on a copier, if needed.
2. Position tracing on surface. Secure with tape.
3. Slide the transfer paper under the tracing with the transfer side facing the surface.
4. Using a stylus, neatly trace over the pattern lines to transfer the lines to the surface.

Painting Tips

- When loading a brush with a different color, but one that is in the same color family, it is preferable to wipe the brush on a damp paper towel to remove excess paint before loading a new color. Avoid rinsing the brush too often in water.

- When loading your brush with a color in a different color family, the brush does not need to be thoroughly cleaned. Simply rinse in water and blot brush on a paper towel to remove excess water. Then load the brush with a new color.

- Sometimes I paint with a "dirty brush." Leaving some of the color in the brush from another element seems to blend the colors together better. For example, if I want to add a reddish tint to a leaf, I will leave a little green in my brush when I load the red so that the colors can "marry."

Finishing Your Piece

A clear finish is needed to protect the painted surface. For wood surfaces, I apply two or more coats of **waterbase varnish** as follows:

1. Let the painting thoroughly dry and cure. Using a **synthetic bristle brush or sponge brush**, apply a coat of brush-on varnish. Let dry.

2. Rub the surface with a piece of a brown paper bag with no printing on it to smooth the surface.

3. Apply a final coat of varnish or a coat of clear **paste wax**.

Flyspecking

Flyspecking adds an aged look to your pieces. To flyspeck, you need an old toothbrush, the paint color of your choice, glazing medium, a palette knife, and a mixing surface such as a palette or a plastic container. (**Photos 1 and 2**)

Photo 1 - Place a small amount of the paint color on your mixing surface. Add glazing medium to paint, Mix with a palette knife to a very thin consistency. Dip the toothbrush in the thin paint.

Photo 2 - Point the toothbrush at your surface and pull your thumb across the bristles to spatter paint over the surface. (You could pull the palette knife across the bristles instead of your thumb.)

Painting Terms

BASECOATING

Preparing and painting your project surface before the decorative painting is applied.

BASIC BRUSH STROKES

Basic brush strokes are done with round and flat brushes. Brush strokes are like the letters of the alphabet. They are easy to learn, but they do require practice. Learning them is very important as they are the basis for all of your painting. For example, if you are painting a flower petal, such as a daisy, you will paint each petal with one brush stroke such as a teardrop. Use as few strokes as possible to paint each part of the design.

COLOR WASH

A color wash is an application of very thin paint. Actually, one could say it is water with just a little color in it that is applied over a painted surface to add a blush of color. A wash can also be made with glazing medium and a bit of color.

CONSISTENCY

Consistency describes the thickness or thinness of the paint. You need different consistencies for different techniques. When you do brush strokes, the paint must be a creamy consistency. When you do line work, the paint must be very thin like the consistency of ink. If the paint is too thick, add a few drops of water to the paint puddle on your palette and mix with a palette knife until the proper consistency is reached.

CONTRAST

Contrast is the sharp difference between two or more colors. When two colors meet, one edge must be light (usually the top edge) and the other edge or shadowed area must be dark. Contrast gives life to your painting.

CURING

When something is dry to the touch, it is not necessarily cured. If something is cured, it is dry all the way through. I often explain curing with this analogy: If you fall down and skin your knee and it bleeds, it's wet. When the scab forms, it's dry. When the new skin grows, it's cured.

I am frequently asked how long it takes a painted piece to cure. There is no right answer – curing depends upon the temperature, air circulation, humidity, the paint color used, and the thinness or thickness of the paint. When a piece is cured, it feels warm and dry to the touch. Curing can take three hours or several weeks.

DOUBLE-LOADING

Double-loading is a technique of loading the brush with two colors of paint. Using two different puddles of paint, load half of the brush with the lighter color and the other half with the darker color. Blend by stroking your brush many, many times on the palette on one side of the brush, then turn the brush over and stroke on the other side. It takes many strokes to prime a brush and get it good and full of paint.

OUTLINING

Most of the time, I outline with a #1 liner brush. (It's possible to outline with the very fine point of any good brush.) When outlining, the brush should be full of paint that has been thinned to the consistency of ink.

STIPPLING

To stipple, you need a brush with a flat tip – a stippling brush, a scruffy brush, or a stencil brush. The brush is loaded, then dabbed up and down on the surface to produce an irregular covering of paint – little dots or specks – from the flat brush tip.

UNDERCOATING

Undercoating is neatly and smoothly painting a design or part of a design solidly on the basecoated project surface. Your strokes, shading, and highlighting will be done on top of this undercoated design.

WASH

See "Color Wash."

BRUSH SKILLS

Using a Round Brush

Round brushes are used primarily for stroking – we seldom blend with them. They come in a variety of sizes. Practice your round brush strokes on the Brush Stroke Worksheet.

LOADING THE BRUSH

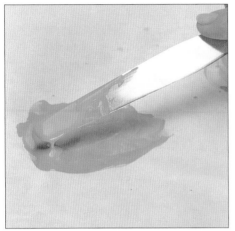

Photo 1. Squeeze paint on your palette. If needed, thin your paint with a thinning medium such as glazing medium or water. Paint should be a creamy consistency.

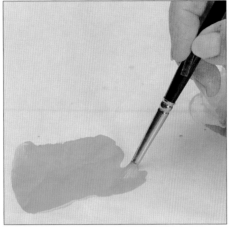

Photo 2. Load brush by picking up paint from the edge of the puddle.

TEARDROP OR POLLIWOG STROKE

Photo 1. Touch on the tip of the brush and apply pressure.

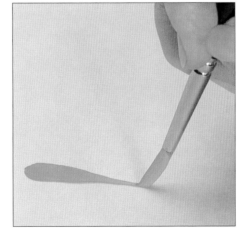

Photo 2. Gradually lift and drag straight down. Turning the brush slightly left or right forces the hairs back together to form a point.

Using a Flat Brush

Flat brushes are designed for brush strokes and blending. They come in many different sizes. Flat brush strokes or any type of stroke may be painted in a single color. It is always a good idea to practice the stroke using a single color before you double-load. These photos show a double-loaded brush, but the procedure is the same if you are using a single color. Practice your flat brush strokes on the Brush Stroke Worksheet that follows.

DOUBLE-LOADING

Double-loading involves loading your brush with two colors. Be sure to thin the paint with water to a flowing consistency and push it with a palette knife to form a neat puddle with a clean edge.

Photo 1. Stroke up against the edge of the light color 30 times, so half of the brush is loaded with paint and the other half is clean.

Photo 2. Turn the brush over and stroke up against the edge of the dark color 20 times.

Photo 3. Blend, blend, blend one side of the brush on your palette.

Photo 4. Turn the brush over and blend, blend, blend on the other side, keeping the dark color in the center and the light color to the outside.

Photo 5. Go back and pick up more light paint on the brush.

Photo 6. Go back to the blending spot on your palette and blend some more.

Photo 7. Go back and pick up some more of the dark color.

Photo 8. Go back to the blending spot on your palette and blend some more. Continue doing this until your brush is really full of paint.

Photo 9. Here is a correctly double-loaded brush. You don't want a space between the two colors; you want them to blend into each other in the center of the brush.

BASIC STROKE

Photo 1. Touch the length of the flat or chisel edge of the brush to your surface.

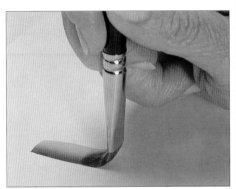

Photo 2. Press the brush down and pull it toward you, holding the pressure steady. Lift the brush smoothly at the end of the stroke.

LINE STROKE

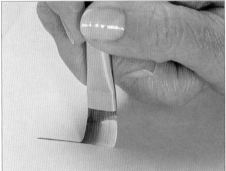

Stand the brush on its flat or chisel edge, perpendicular to the orientation of the basic flat stroke. The handle should point straight up toward the ceiling. Pull the brush toward you. Don't press the brush down, as this would thicken and distort the line.

Using a Liner Brush

Liner brushes are the long, thinner members of the round brush family. Their bristles come to a wonderful point. Liner brushes are used for fine line work. Practice your liner brush strokes on the Brush Stroke Worksheet.

LOADING

Photo 1. Thin paint with water until it is the consistency of ink.

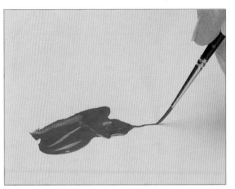

Photo 2. Fill the brush full of paint by pulling it through paint at edge. Twist the brush as you pull it out of puddle (this will form a nice pointed tip). When you are using the brush hold it straight up.

TEARDROP STROKE

Fill brush with paint of a thin consistency; touch, apply pressure, begin pulling and lifting, then drag to a point.

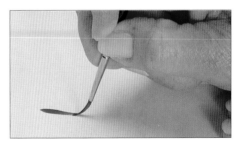

CURLICUES & SQUIGGLES

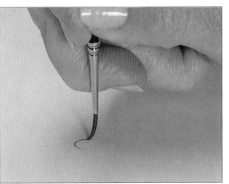

Photo 1. Stand the brush on its point with the handle pointing straight up toward the ceiling.

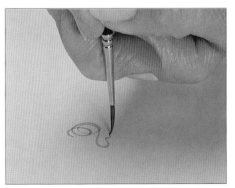

Photo 2. Slowly move the brush to paint loopy Ms and Ws. Practice several times on your page. Make as many variations as you wish.

Round Brush Strokes

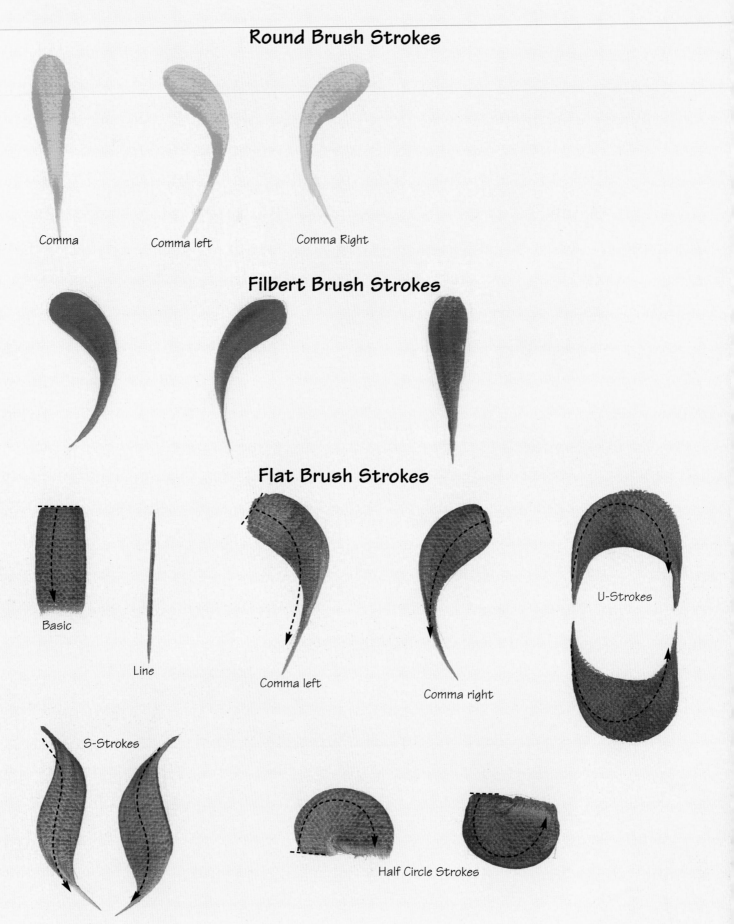

Comma   Comma left   Comma Right

Filbert Brush Strokes

Flat Brush Strokes

Basic

Line

Comma left

Comma right

U-Strokes

S-Strokes

Half Circle Strokes

Double-Loaded Brush Strokes (using a #12 flat brush)

Basic

Line

Comma left

Comma right

U-Strokes

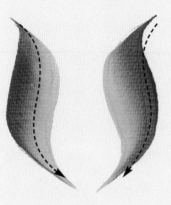

Half Circle Strokes

S-Strokes

Liner Brush Strokes

Use a very thin paint
and a full brush. Move
the brush slowly.

PAINTING TECHNIQUES

Shading & Highlighting with Floating

Floating is flowing color on a surface. This technique is used for adding the shading and highlighting to design elements. Before floating, undercoat the area. Let dry. Add a second or even a third coat, if necessary. Let dry. Our example shows shading and highlighting floated on a leaf that has been undercoated in a gray-green (bayberry) color.

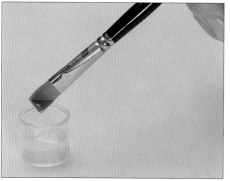

Photo 1. Fill your brush with floating medium. Your brush size is determined by the design.

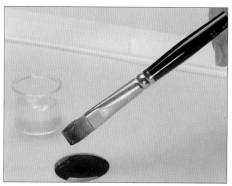

Photo 2. Fill one side of the brush with the shading color by stroking up against the edge of a puddle of paint.

Photo 3. On a matte surface, such as tracing paper or wet palette paper, blend, blend, blend on one side of the brush.

Photo 4. Then turn the brush over and blend, blend, blend on the other side. Keep the paint in the center. Be sure the brush is good and full of paint and that the color graduates through the brush from dark to medium to clear.

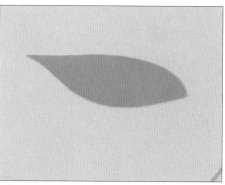

Photo 5. The floating of shading and highlighting will be done atop the undercoating. Here the leaf was undercoated with bayberry.

Photo 6. Float on the shading to the edge of the design (here, a leaf), with the dark side of the brush towards the outside of the design. Let dry. Repeat the process, if desired, to deepen the color.

Photo 7. Highlighting is floated on the opposite side of the design, using the same technique as shading but using a light color.

Option: Water can be used in place of floating medium. Dip the brush in water and blot by gently pulling the brush along the edge of your water basin.

Blending

In this book, I have done a very easy type of blending. First, neatly and carefully undercoat and let dry. Blending medium, which allows you to easily blend colors together, is used for this technique.

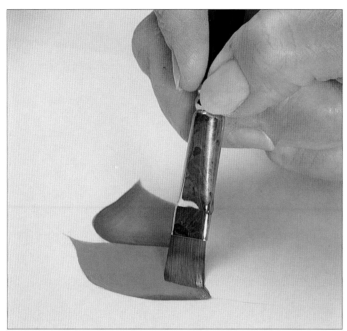

Photo 1. Float on the shadows. Let dry.

Photo 2. Add a small amount of blending medium.

Photo 3. Add the colors you wish to blend on top of the wet medium.

Photo 4. Lightly blend or move the colors together, using an extremely light touch. If you are heavy handed, you will wipe all the color away. If this happens, let the blending medium dry and cure and begin again *or* remove the color before it dries, add more blending medium, and begin again.

Painting a Quick & Easy Leaf

This leaf works nicely for many of the projects in this book. It is the leaf used for the lilacs, sunflowers, and lemons. The Leaf Worksheet illustrates the technique, step by step.

PALETTE OF COLORS

Artist Pigment Acrylic Paints:

Green Dark

Green Light

Green Medium

Green Umber

Acrylic Craft Paint:

Payne's Gray

Titanium White

Old Ivy

BRUSHES

Brush size depends upon the size of the leaf. I used:

#12 Flat

OTHER SUPPLIES

In addition to the Basic Supplies listed on page 29, you will need:

Blending medium

INSTRUCTIONS

Refer to the Leaf Worksheet, opposite.

1. Undercoat the leaf with Old Ivy. (Fig. 1) Two or three coats will be needed to cover. Let dry and cure.
2. Double-load your brush with water and Green Umber (or a shadow color of your choice). Blend on the palette so the color blends through the brush from dark to medium to light. Float the shadow color at the base and shadow areas of the leaf. (Fig. 2) Let dry and cure.
3. Apply a small amount of blending medium over the leaf. (Fig. 3)
4. Wipe the brush. Add Green Umber, Green Dark, Green Medium, and Titanium White. (Fig. 4)
5. Wipe the brush. Using a very light touch, blend from the base of the leaf out toward the edges. (Fig. 5) Lift the brush as you pull toward the edges, letting it take off like an airplane lifting off the runway. You don't want to pull the color out over the edges. If needed, apply more blending medium and paint.
6. Lightly blend from the outside edges back toward the base, merging the colors lightly together, following the shape of the leaf. (Fig. 6) If you want a darker leaf, use more of the shadow color or Green Dark. For a lighter leaf, use more Green Light and Titanium White. ❏

Leaf Worksheet

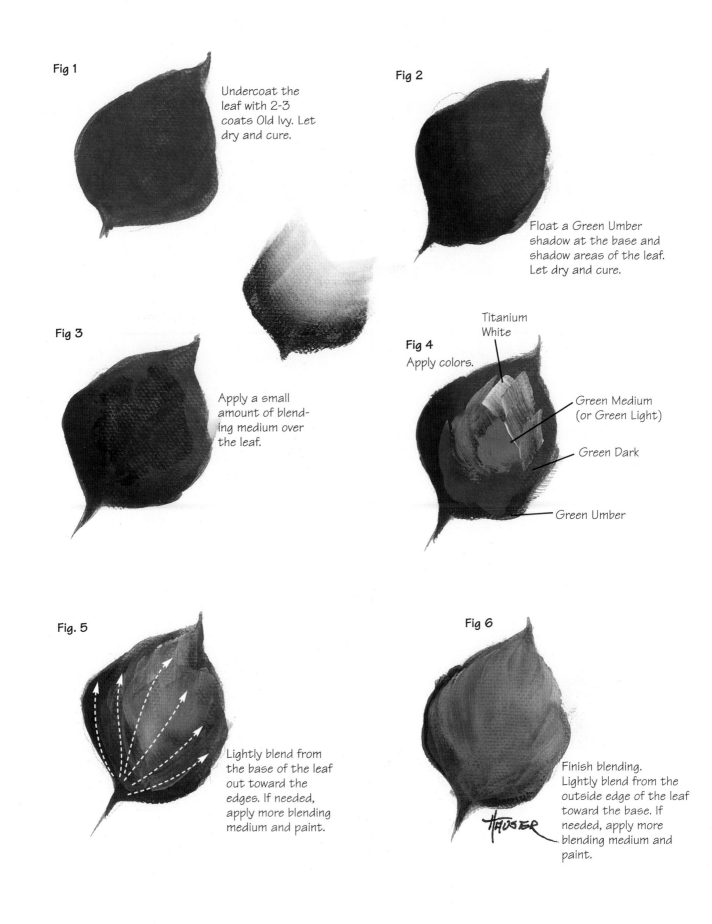

Fig 1

Undercoat the leaf with 2-3 coats Old Ivy. Let dry and cure.

Fig 2

Float a Green Umber shadow at the base and shadow areas of the leaf. Let dry and cure.

Fig 3

Apply a small amount of blending medium over the leaf.

Fig 4
Apply colors.

Titanium White

Green Medium (or Green Light)

Green Dark

Green Umber

Fig. 5

Lightly blend from the base of the leaf out toward the edges. If needed, apply more blending medium and paint.

Fig 6

Finish blending. Lightly blend from the outside edge of the leaf toward the base. If needed, apply more blending medium and paint.

28

THE PROJECTS

The projects in this book can be painted on a variety of surfaces and the design motifs can be used to create practically endless variations. Each project section includes a list of paint colors and supplies, step-by-step instructions, painting worksheets with numerous examples, and patterns. You'll also find how-to photographs for painting techniques and lots of tips and advice. Enjoy!

Refer to the previous Basic Supplies section and collect all the necessary supplies as listed there before you begin a painting project. You will need the following items for painting any of the projects:

- Acrylic Paints
- Painting Mediums
- Artist Brushes
- Water basin for brushes
- Palette and palette knife
- Sponge brushes if basecoating your piece is necessary
- Sandpaper

- Tack rag
- Brown paper bags
- Tracing paper and pencil
- Chalk or graphite paper
- Stylus
- Cotton rags or paper towels
- Varnish

Palms & Monkeys

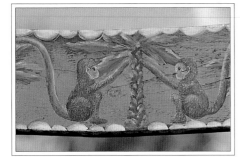

Side Chair

I liked the worn look and the wonderful blue color of the paint on this wooden chair. I painted a monkey-and-palm tree design on the chair back for an English Colonial look. Because this look is so popular, I had no trouble finding a cushion for the chair with fabric that complemented my painted design.

PALETTE OF COLORS

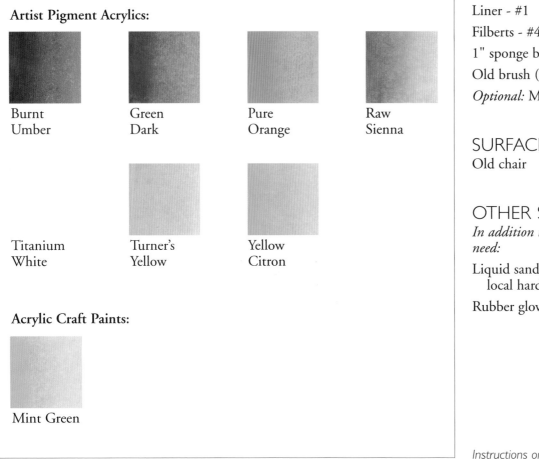

Artist Pigment Acrylics:

Burnt Umber

Green Dark

Pure Orange

Raw Sienna

Titanium White

Turner's Yellow

Yellow Citron

Acrylic Craft Paints:

Mint Green

BRUSHES

Flats - #4, #8, #10, #12

Liner - #1

Filberts - #4, #12

1" sponge brush

Old brush (for stippling)

Optional: Mop brush

SURFACE

Old chair

OTHER SUPPLIES

In addition to the Basic Supplies, you'll need:

Liquid sanding preparation (from your local hardware store)

Rubber gloves

Instructions on page 32

PREPARATION

1. Sand the chair, if needed. Wipe with a tack cloth.
2. Wipe with a liquid sanding preparation. (Be sure to wear rubber gloves.) Let dry thoroughly.
3. *Option:* If you don't like the background color or the chair has not been painted, paint the chair with the color of your choice. Let dry and cure.
4. Transfer the pattern, using white or gray graphite paper.
5. Unless the chair is painted white, undercoat the monkeys with Titanium White. Let dry.
6. Paint the scalloped borders freehand, using a #12 filbert brush with Titanium White. See the Palms & Monkeys Worksheet, and use the photo as a guide for placement.

PAINTING THE DESIGN

This design is painted using color washes (pigment + water).

Palm Trees:

See the Palms & Monkeys Worksheet. The figure numbers refer to those on the worksheet.

1. Double load a #10 flat brush with Green Dark and Yellow Citron. Using a scribble stroke, form the fronds. (Fig. 1)
2. Deepen the color and fill in the fronds with Green Dark. (Fig. 1)
3. Highlight the fronds with Yellow Citron (Fig. 1) and Mint Green (Fig. 2).
4. Pull in stalks on the fronds with Raw Sienna on the chisel edge of a flat brush. (Fig. 2)
5. Dip the brush in water and sideload with Burnt Umber. Paint the trunk. (Fig. 1) Let dry thoroughly.
6. Using a #4 filbert brush with Turner's Yellow and Raw Sienna, highlight the tree trunk. (Fig. 2)

Monkeys:

See the Monkeys Worksheet. The figure numbers refer to those on the worksheet.

1. Wash the monkey with Raw Sienna, leaving the face white. (Fig. 1) Let dry.
2. Shade with floats of Raw Sienna. (Fig. 1) Let dry.
3. Deepen shading with floats of Burnt Umber. (Fig. 2) Let dry.
4. For texture, stipple the monkeys' bodies with Burnt Umber and Turner's Yellow, using an old brush.
5. Shade the face with Raw Sienna.
6. Highlight the face and body with Titanium White + Turner's Yellow.
7. Paint a Burnt Umber dot for the eye, using a #1 liner brush. Let dry. Add a small highlight of Titanium White.

Borders:

1. Using a #12 flat brush, shade the upper borders on the back of the chair with floats of Pure Orange and the lower borders with floats of Raw Sienna. Let dry.
2. Add smaller floats of Titanium White. Soften with a #12 filbert or a mop brush. Let dry.

FINISH

1. Apply three or more coats of varnish. Let dry.
2. Rub with a piece of brown paper bag with no printing on it to smooth the surface of the wood. Wipe with a tack cloth.
3. Apply a final coat of varnish and let dry. ❏

Palms & Monkeys Worksheet

Fig. 1

(1) "Scribbled" leaves, using double-loaded washes of Green Dark and Yellow Citron.

(4) Highlights with Yellow Citron.

(5) Trunk painted with Burnt Umber, using a filbert brush.

(2) Color deepened with Green Dark.

(3) Borders painted with Titanium White, using a large filbert brush.

Fig. 2

(4) Border with floats of Pure Orange.

(2) Stalks painted with Raw Sienna.

(1) Highlights with Mint Green.

(3) Raw Sienna highlights on trunk.

(5) Border floated with Raw Sienna.

Monkeys Worksheet

Fig. 1

(1) Body washed with Raw Sienna.

(2) Shading on face and body with floats of Raw Sienna.

(3) Eye painted with Burnt Umber.

Fig. 2

(1) Shading deepened with floats of Burnt Umber.

(4) Highlight eye with Titanium White.

(2) Texture stippled with Burnt Umber and Turner's Yellow.

(3) Highlighting with Turner's Yellow + Titanium White.

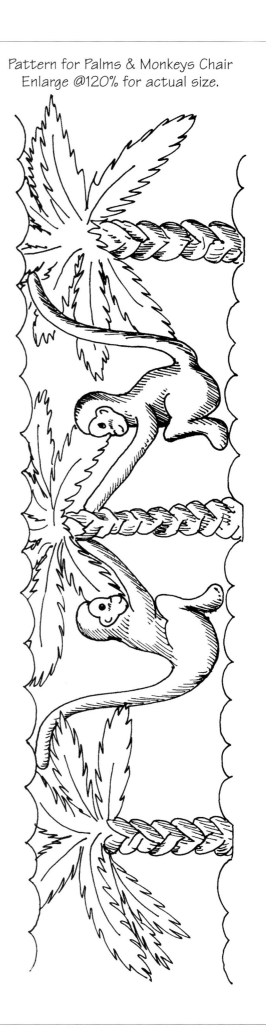

Pattern for Palms & Monkeys Chair
Enlarge @120% for actual size.

Gingham & Geraniums

Round Table

This table was painted white when I purchased it. I sanded it lightly to create an aged look, then decorated the top with red geraniums. A painted gingham effect borders the design, and the turned pedestal is trimmed with the design colors.

PALETTE OF COLORS

Artist Pigment Acrylics:

Green Dark

Green Medium

Green Umber

Green Light

Payne's Gray

Red Light

Titanium White

True Burgundy

Yellow Citron

Yellow Light

Acrylic Craft Paints:

Apple Spice

Clover

BRUSHES

Flats - #2, #4, #6, #8, #12, #14

Liner - #1

Sponge brush

SURFACE

Round pedestal table (This one is 16-1/2" in diameter.)

OTHER SUPPLIES

In addition to the Basic Supplies, you'll need:

Floating medium

Blending medium

Glazing medium

Liquid sandpaper

Transparent tape or painter's tape, 3/4" wide (for masking)

Rubber gloves

Instructions follow on page 38

continued from page 36

PREPARATION

1. Sand the table. Wipe with a tack cloth.

2. Wipe with a liquid sanding preparation. Wear rubber gloves and follow the package directions. Let dry thoroughly.

3. Neatly trace and transfer your design using colored chalk or a used sheet of gray graphite paper (so the lines won't be too dark).

4. Double load a large flat brush with glazing medium and just a little Payne's Gray. Apply this around the outside edges of the geraniums and stems. Let dry.

CREATING THE GINGHAM BORDER

1. Apply strips of tape to the entire area to be painted, placing strips side by side in one direction. Remove every other strip, exposing the surface. (**photo 1**)

2. Paint the stripes made by removing the tape with thinned Apple Spice. (**photo 2**) Remove the rest of the tape. Let dry completely.

3. Place strips of tape in the opposite direction (90 degrees from the first strips), side by side. Remove every other strip.

4. Paint the stripes made by removing the tape with thinned Apple Spice to create the gingham look. Notice that where the stripes cross, the paint is darker. (**photo 3**). Remove the rest of the tape. Let dry completely.

5. Fill your liner brush with Clover thinned with water to an ink-like consistency. Move the brush slowly and carefully to paint the line. Don't worry about it being perfect – hand painting isn't perfect. Let the paint dry and apply a second coat.

Continued on page 42

THE GINGHAM BORDER

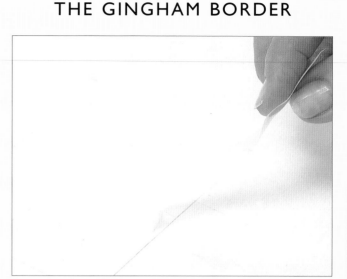

Photo 1 - Applying tape to the surface

Photo 2 - Painting the stripes in one direction

Photo 3 - Painting the second set of stripes

Geraniums Worksheet

Fig. 1:

Fig. 2:

Stroke pattern for flowers.

Stroke medium value petals with Apple Spice + Titanium White, working in blending gel and Apple Spice, wet-into-wet.

Stroke petals with Apple Spice for the dark shadow flowers.

Apply blending gel to leaves, then colors.

Green Light

Green Dark + Payne's Gray

Titanium White

Green Umber + Payne's Gray

Green Medium

Green Medium

True Burgundy

True Burgundy

Titanium White

Green Light

Green Umber + Payne's Gray

Add shadows with Green Umber + Green Dark.

Undercoat leaves with Clover.

Undercoat flowers with Apple Spice.

Clover

40

Fig. 4:

Dot centers with Yellow Light and Yellow Citron.

Paint curlicues with Green Umber.

Fig. 3:

Paint Titanium White flowers over the wet medium value flowers.

Lightly blend leaves from stem out, then from edges in. Add more paint and blending gel, if needed.

Paint buds with Red Light. Shade with True Burgundy.

Shade stems with Green Umber + Payne's Gray.

Continued form page 38

PAINTING THE DESIGN

See the Geraniums Worksheet. The figure numbers refer to those on the worksheet.

Leaves:

1. Neatly undercoat the leaves with Clover. Three coats will be needed to cover. Let the paint dry between each application. (Fig. 1)

2. Apply shadows and folds in the leaves by floating on Green Umber + Green Dark (3:1) with floating medium in brush. Let dry. Float a second or third time to deepen the shadows. (Fig. 1) Let dry.

3. To complete the leaves, work one leaf at a time. Start with the ones underneath and work toward the top leaves. Apply blending medium, and then apply the colors shown on the worksheet. (Fig. 2) Wipe the brush and blend, using a light touch and following the natural curve of the leaf. (Fig. 3)

Stems:

1. Paint the stems with Clover. (Fig. 1)

2. Shade with Green Umber to which you have added a tiny touch of Payne's Gray. (Fig. 3)

3. Highlight with Green Light.

Geraniums:

1. Undercoat the geraniums with two or more coats of Apple Spice. (Fig. 1) Be sure you have uneven edges on the flowers.

2. Using a #2 or #4 flat brush full of Apple Spice, paint the petals for the dark shadow flowers. (Fig. 2) Let dry.

3. Apply a small amount of blending medium to the clump and more Apple Spice. (Fig. 2)

4. Mix Apple Spice + Titanium White (3:1). Paint the medium value flowers as shown on the worksheet, Fig. 2.

5. Quickly wipe the brush. Pick up Titanium White and paint just a few flowers on top of the wet medium value flowers. (Fig. 3)

6. Add tiny dots of Yellow Light and Yellow Citron for the centers. (Fig. 4)

Buds:

1. Paint buds with Red Light.

2. Shade with True Burgundy.

Curlicues:

Fill a #1 liner brush with thinned Green Umber and paint the curlicues.

Trim:

Accent the pedestal with colors from the design, using the photo as a guide for placement. Let dry and cure.

FINISH

1. Varnish with three or more coats of varnish. Let dry.

2. Rub with a piece of brown paper bag with no printing on it to smooth the raised nap of the wood.

3. Apply a final coat of varnish. Let dry. ❏

Pattern for Gingham & Geraniums Round Table
Enlarge @200% for actual size.

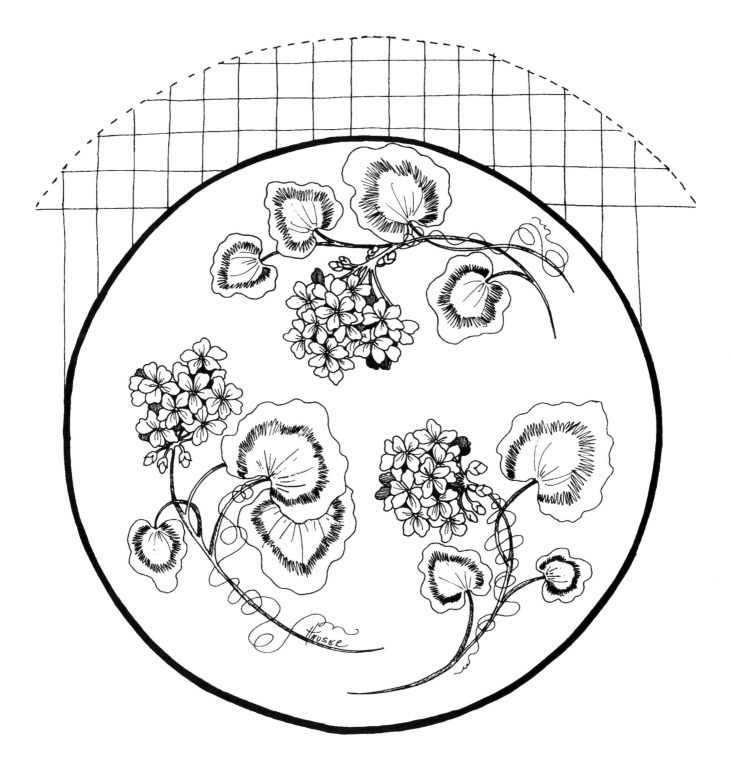

Lollipop Roses

Desk & Chair

PALETTE OF COLORS

Artist Pigment Acrylics:

Green
Light

Green
Medium

Green
Umber

Titanium
White

Acrylic Craft Paints:

Apple
Spice

Clover

There are so many beautiful old pieces of furniture that are cast aside. This desk and chair are two of those treasures. A wonderful thing about old furniture is finding a piece with turnings – they are great places for applying colorful accents.

Both the desk and the chair were already painted white when I purchased them from a used furniture store. I created a lattice design for the desktop and a picket-and-wire fence motif that is used on the desk drawer, the chair back, and the edge of the chair seat. I call these easy to paint roses "lollipop roses" because they remind me of those old-fashioned brightly colored lollipops that had a spiral design.

BRUSHES
Flats - #4, #8, #12, #16
Liner - #1
Round - #3

SURFACES
An old desk
An old chair

OTHER SUPPLIES
In addition to the Basic Supplies, you'll need:

Blending medium

Floating medium

Wood glue

Sandpaper

Liquid sanding preparation

100% cotton rags

Piece of brown paper bag with no printing on it

Clear cellophane tape or painter's tape, 1" wide

2 wooden balls (to decorate the back of the chair)

Rubber gloves

Continued on next page

PREPARATION

1. Sand the chair and desk, as needed. Wipe with a rag.

2. Wipe with a liquid sanding preparation. Let dry thoroughly.

CREATING THE LATTICE DESIGN ON THE DESK

1. Decide how big you want the lattice panel to be in the top of the desk. Measure, mark, and mask off with tape, pressing edges securely.

2. Cover the entire lattice area with strips of tape, placing the tape pieces diagonally in one direction, side by side. Remove every third strip of tape.

3. Using a wide brush, neatly apply one smooth coat of Green Medium to create the lattice in one direction. (**photo 1**) Let dry.

4. Apply a second coat of Green Medium over the first. Remove all the tape. Let dry and cure thoroughly. *Tip: Be sure the first portion of the lattice is completely dry and cured before proceeding. If it's not, you could lift the paint with the tape for the second portion.*

5. Apply tape in the opposite diagonal direction, covering the entire lattice area. Remove every third piece of tape. (**photo 2**)

6. Apply two coats of Green Medium. (**Photo 3**) Let the paint dry between coats. Carefully lift off the tape. Let dry and cure completely.

7. Remove the tape from the outside edges of the lattice area. Mask off a 1/4" border to frame the lattice.

8. Paint the border with two coats of Apple Spice. Let dry. Remove tape.

Continued on page 48

THE LATTICE DESIGN

Photo 1 - Painting the lattice in one direction

Photo 2 - Removing every third strip of tape

Photo 3 - Painting the lattice in the other direction

continued from page 46

PAINTING THE DESIGN

See the Lollipop Roses Worksheet on pages 52 and 53. The figure numbers refer to those on the worksheets.

Transferring the Designs:

Using colored chalk or an old worn piece of gray graphite paper, neatly trace and transfer the lollipop rose designs and the picket fence designs to the desk and chair, using the project photos as guides for placement.

Leaves:

Paint the back (underneath) leaves first and work forward. Complete one leaf at a time.

1. Undercoat the leaves with three coats of Clover. (Fig. 1) Let the paint dry between each application.
2. Using as large a brush as you feel comfortable with, apply a shadow to the base of the leaves by floating on Green Umber with floating medium in brush. (Fig. 2) Let dry.
3. Apply a small amount of blending medium over the leaf (careful, not too much!).
4. Apply a little Green Umber at the base of the leaf. (Fig. 3)
5. Apply Green Light to the remaining portion of the leaf. (Fig. 3)
6. Wipe the brush and blend the two colors where they meet. (Fig. 3)

Lollipop Roses:

Remember you can always wipe off and do it again if you are not satisfied.

1. Using a large flat brush, undercoat each rose with three applications of Apple Spice. (**photo 1**) Let the paint dry between each coat.
2. Working one rose at a time, coat the rose with blending medium. (**photo 2**)
3. Apply more Apple Spice to the rose. (**photo 3**)
4. Make a pink mix with Titanium White + Apple Spice (4:1). (Fig. 3) Thin this with a little water to a flowing consistency.
5. Fill a #3 round brush with the light pink mixture. Beginning at the outside edge, paint a spiral toward the center. (**photo 4**) Finish the spiral at the center of the rose. (**photo 5**) Let the paint dry.

Curlicues:

1. Mix Green Light + a tiny touch of Green Umber. Thin the mixture with water to an ink-like consistency. Fill a #1 liner brush with the mixture.
2. Stand the brush on its point, and neatly and slowly paint the curls and swirls. (Fig. 4) Let dry.

Continued on page 50

PAINTING LOLLIPOP ROSES

Photo 1 - Undercoating the rose

Photo 2 - Apply blending medium

Photo 3 - Applying more Apple Spice

Photo 4 - Painting the spiral with a liner brush

Photo 5 - Finishing the spiral

WIPING OFF

If you aren't satisfied with something you just painted, remember you can always wipe off and do it again. *Tip:* When you wipe off something, wipe from the outside edge in toward the center rather than from the inside out to avoid smearing the paint on the rest of the design.

continued from page 48

Fence Trim:

1. Paint the fence pickets using a #4 flat brush full of Green Medium. (Fig. 5) Two coats are needed for coverage. (Fig. 6) Let dry.

2. Paint the wire using the #1 liner brush full of Green Medium thinned to an ink-like consistency. (Fig. 6)

Color Accents:

Accent the desk and chair with touches of Apple Spice and Green Medium, using the photo as a guide for placement. Three coats of Apple Spice and two coats of Green Medium will be needed to cover.

FINISH

1. Glue the wooden balls to the top of the chair. Let dry and cure.

2. Apply three or more coats of varnish. Let dry.

3. Rub with a piece of brown paper bag with no printing on it to smooth the raised nap of the wood.

4. Apply a final coat of varnish and let dry.

5. *Option:* To protect the top of the desk, have a piece of glass cut to fit the top. Use spacers between the desk and the glass to keep the paint and varnish from sticking to the glass. ❑

TIPS FOR LINE WORK & CURLICUES

1. Fill the brush good and full of paint thinned to an ink-like consistency.

2. Hold the brush so the handle points straight up toward the ceiling.

3. Move the brush slowly and allow the paint time to flow from the hairs of the brush.

Tip: Be sure you can see the brush touching the surface. Often people tell me the paint skips because they cannot actually see the tip of the brush touching the surface they are painting.

Lollipop Roses Worksheet

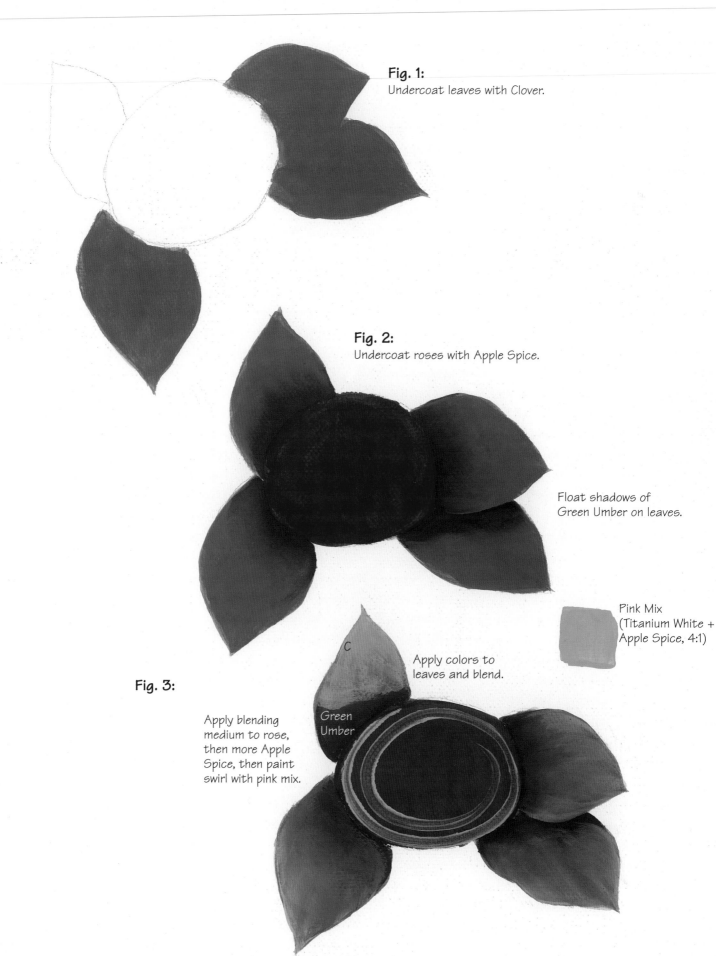

Fig. 1:
Undercoat leaves with Clover.

Fig. 2:
Undercoat roses with Apple Spice.

Float shadows of
Green Umber on leaves.

Pink Mix
(Titanium White +
Apple Spice, 4:1)

Apply colors to
leaves and blend.

Fig. 3:

Apply blending
medium to rose,
then more Apple
Spice, then paint
swirl with pink mix.

C

Green
Umber

Fig. 4:
The completed rose.

Fig. 5:
Paint fence pickets with Green Medium.

Fig. 6:

Second coat of Green Medium.

Wire painted with Green Medium that is thinned to an ink-like consistency.

Patterns for Lollipop Roses Desk Top
Enlarge @125% for actual size.

Pattern for
Chair Seat Edge
Enlarge @135%
for actual size.

Pattern for Desk Drawer Front
Enlarge @135% for actual size.

Pattern for Chair Back
Enlarge @135% for actual size.

Pattern for Lollipop Roses Chair Seat
(Actual Size)

Toile Roses & Quail

Square Side Table

This wonderful little table was painted white when I found it. If your table is not already painted, all you need to do is apply a coat of white paint. This project uses only three paint colors — two blues (periwinkle and light periwinkle) and white. The style and motifs are like those found on toile wallpaper and fabrics.

PALETTE OF COLORS

Acrylic Craft Paints:

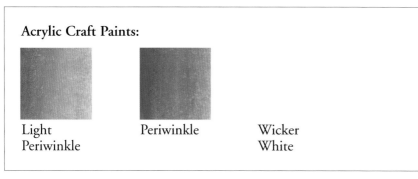

Light Periwinkle

Periwinkle

Wicker White

BRUSHES

Flats - #2, #4, #8, #10, #12, #14

Liner - #1

Filbert - #4

SURFACE

Square table with a shelf

OTHER SUPPLIES

In addition to the Basic Supplies, you'll need:

Blending medium

Floating medium

Liquid sandpaper

Plastic wrap

Painter's tape

Compass

Rubber gloves

PREPARATION

1. Lightly sand the table for a distressed look. Wipe with a tack cloth.
2. Wipe with a liquid sanding preparation. Let dry thoroughly. Be sure to wear rubber gloves and follow the directions on the product.
3. Paint the lower shelf, the edges of the lower shelf, and the edges of the table top with Periwinkle Blue. Use the photo as a guide and adapt the idea to fit your table.

CREATING THE MOTTLED BACKGROUND

1. Mix Periwinkle with water (6 parts water to a tiny touch of Periwinkle) on a palette. Crumple a piece of plastic wrap in your hand and pounce in the thinned paint. Lightly blot on a rag. Using the plastic wrap as an applicator, dab the thinned Paint all over the table top. Let dry.
2. Use a compass to apply a circle 7-1/4" in diameter. (**photo 1**)
3. Neatly trace and transfer the design with an old piece of graphite (or a sheet of new graphite wiped with a cloth to take away some of the harshness).
4. Using a liner brush full of thinned Periwinkle, outline the circle. (**photo 2**)
5. Using the liner brush, paint tiny commas strokes around the outer edge.
6. Where the comma strokes begin and end, add dots of Periwinkle, using the handle end of the brush to apply them.

Continued on page 60

continued from page 58

PAINTING THE DESIGN

See the Toile Worksheet. The figure numbers refer to those on the worksheet.

Roses & Leaves:

Paint the small leaves using the #4 filbert. Use larger brushes for the larger leaves. Use a #4 flat for the smaller roses, a #6 for the medium roses, and a #10 for the larger roses.

1. Paint the shadows with Periwinkle. (Fig. 1) Let dry.
2. Working one leaf or flower at a time, apply a dab of blending medium.
3. Apply Wicker White and a little more Periwinkle.
4. Neatly blend where the two colors meet each other. (Fig. 2)
5. Outline using a liner brush full of thinned Periwinkle. (Fig. 3)

Grass:

1. Fill the #1 liner brush with thinned, ink-like Periwinkle and very slowly paint the blades of grass. (**photo 3**) *Option:* Use the chisel edge of a flat brush.
2. Highlight with Wicker White.

Quail:

1. With Periwinkle, float dark shading (with floating medium in brush) to outline the quail's body and wing and to paint the strokes on the wings and chest. (**photos 4 and 5**) See Figs. 4 and 5 on the Toile Worksheet. Let dry.
2. Mix a Light Periwinkle wash (water plus a touch of color) and brush lightly over the bird. (Fig. 5)
3. Paint the Head feathers, beak, feet, and eye, using the liner brush full of thinned Periwinkle. (Fig. 6)
4. Add a tiny Wicker White dot to highlight the eye. (Fig. 6) Let dry and cure.

FINISH

1. Apply three or more coats of varnish. Let dry.
2. Rub with a piece of brown paper bag with no printing on it to smooth the surface. Wipe with a tack cloth.
3. Apply a final coat of varnish and let dry. ❑

THE TOILE DESIGN

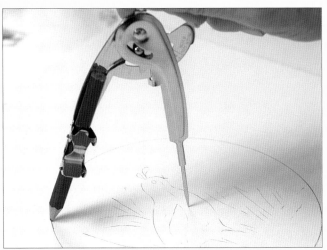

Photo 1 - Using a compass to make the circle

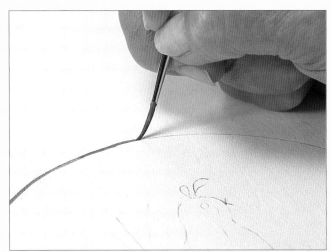

Photo 2 - Painting the circle with a liner brush

Photo 3 - Painting the blades of grass

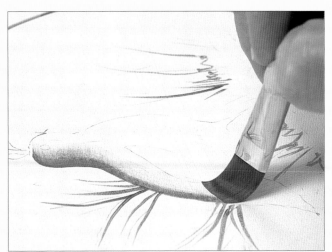

Photo 4 - Floating the outline of the quail with floating medium plus color in brush.

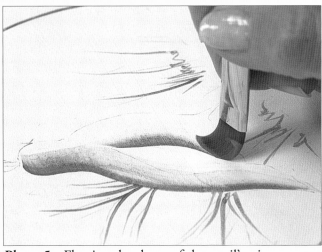

Photo 5 - Floating the shape of the quail's wing

Top view of Toile Roses & Quail Table

Closeup view of toile design.

Pattern for central motif for Toile Roses & Quail Table
(Actual Size)

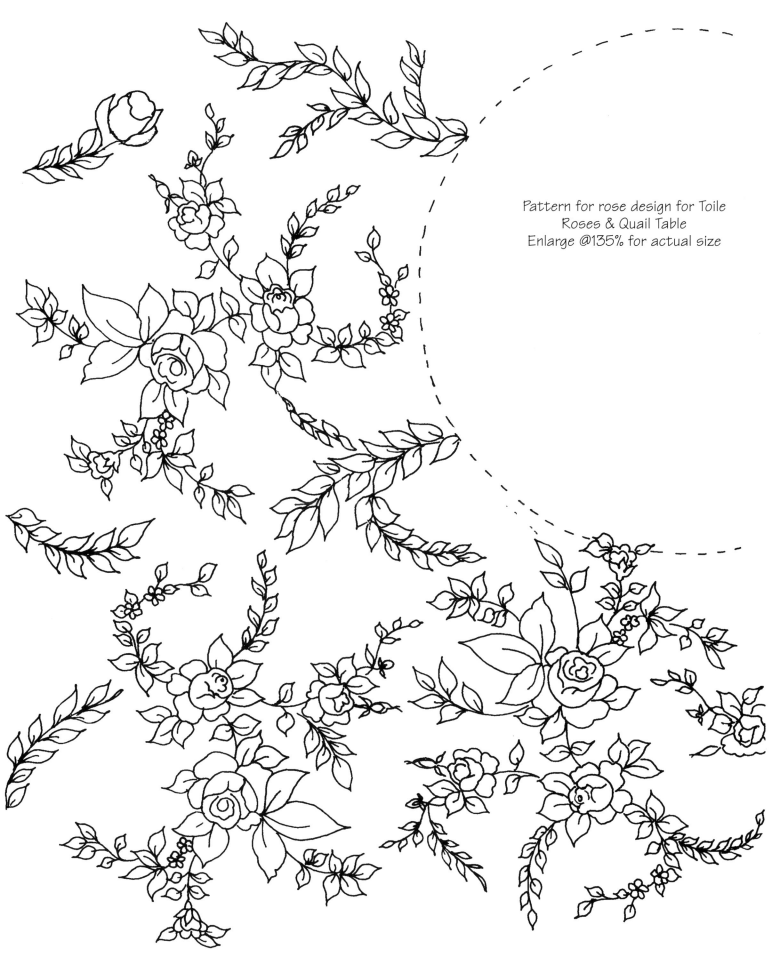

Pattern for rose design for Toile
Roses & Quail Table
Enlarge @135% for actual size

Pears & Grapes

Shelf Unit

This simple bookcase is great for storing all kinds of things, including books! I painted it so it could be used in the kitchen to store cookbooks and a wonderful old jar collection. As a background for the pear-and-grape motifs, I chose a light gray-green and accented the piece with periwinkle blue. I antiqued the carved border areas at the top and bottom with a glaze made from the periwinkle color.

PALETTE OF COLORS

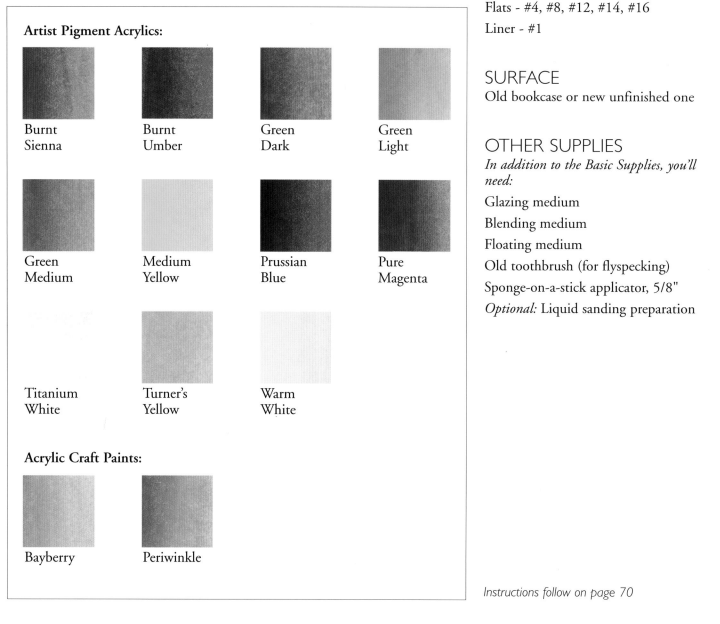

Artist Pigment Acrylics:

Burnt Sienna

Burnt Umber

Green Dark

Green Light

Green Medium

Medium Yellow

Prussian Blue

Pure Magenta

Titanium White

Turner's Yellow

Warm White

Acrylic Craft Paints:

Bayberry

Periwinkle

BRUSHES
Flats - #4, #8, #12, #14, #16
Liner - #1

SURFACE
Old bookcase or new unfinished one

OTHER SUPPLIES
In addition to the Basic Supplies, you'll need:

Glazing medium

Blending medium

Floating medium

Old toothbrush (for flyspecking)

Sponge-on-a-stick applicator, 5/8"

Optional: Liquid sanding preparation

Instructions follow on page 70

continued from page 68

behind the pears or the grapes.

PREPARATION

Basecoating:

1. Sand the bookcase and wipe with a tack cloth.
2. If previously painted, wipe with a liquid sanding preparation.
3. Basecoat with two or more coats of Bayberry. Let dry between coats.
4. Paint tops of shelves and trim areas (e.g., edges of shelves) with Periwinkle. Apply as many coats as needed for full coverage. Use the photo as a guide for color placement.

Antiquing:

1. Make an antiquing glaze by combining glazing medium and Periwinkle (3:1). Brush the glaze mixture over the carved areas.
2. Wipe with a soft rag. Let dry.

PAINTING THE DESIGN

Neatly trace and transfer the design to painting surface.

Leaves:

See the Leaves Worksheet. The figure numbers refer to those on the worksheet.

1. Undercoat with two coats Green Medium. Let dry.
2. Float on Green Dark at the base, with floating medium in brush.
3. Float Green Dark on the dark side. Let dry.
4. Working one leaf at a time, apply blending medium, then colors – a little Titanium White along the light side of the leaf, Green Light in the middle of the leaf, and Green Dark at the base of the leaf. Lightly blend the colors where they meet.
5. Using a liner brush, add a vein with thinned Green Dark.

Stems:

See the Pears & Grapes Worksheet.

1. Undercoat the stem with three coats of a light brown mix (Burnt Umber + Titanium White, 1:4). (Fig. 6) Let dry and cure.
2. Working one section at a time, apply a little blending medium to the stem and reapply the light brown mixture. Wipe the brush. Double load with the brown mixture and Burnt Umber. Shade down the left or dark side of the stem. Add a highlight of Titanium White. (Fig. 7)
3. Wipe the brush and pull the dark across to the light and the light to the dark. (Fig. 8) Use a light touch.
4. Apply a Burnt Umber shadow where the stem goes

Pears:

See the Pears & Grapes Worksheet.

1. Undercoat with three coats Turner's Yellow. (Fig. 2) Let the paint dry and cure.
2. Using a large flat brush, float Burnt Sienna on the dark side. (Fig. 3) Let dry and cure.
3. Float Green Light on the light side. (Fig. 3) Let dry and cure.
4. Apply blending medium to the pear and apply the colors shown on the worksheet. (Fig. 4) Wipe the brush and blend. Add more paint and blending medium as desired. Use a light touch when blending and follow the pear's natural curves. (If you don't like what you've painted, let the paint dry and cure, then start over.)
5. Double load a small flat brush with blending medium and Burnt Sienna. Paint the indentation where the stem joins the pear. (Fig. 5) (It's a little s-stroke.) *Tip:* It's easier to create this little stroke if you turn the pear upside down to paint it.

Grapes:

See the Pears & Grapes Worksheet, Fig. 1. On the worksheet I've done a dark, a medium, and a light grape. They were all painted completely with the round sponge-on-a-stick applicator. Practice on paper or other surface before painting your project.

1. Dip the sponge applicator in blending medium and blot on a rag.
2. Make a light blue mix (Titanium White + Prussian Blue, 5:1) and a lavender mix (Pure Magenta + Titanium White, 1:5). Undercoat the grapes in one or the other of these mixes. To do this, dip the round applicator in the color; blot, blot, blot on a rag; twist the applicator as you press down on the surface and gently wiggle it from side to side. You may have to go over it two or three times. You may even need to let the paint dry between the applications. This is the undercoat.
3. Add shading and highlighting colors to the grapes, using the worksheet as a guide. Have fun playing with the colors. Paint the grapes in different values – some dark, some medium, and some light.

Curlicues:

Fill a #1 liner brush with thinned Burnt Umber + a touch of Burnt Sienna. Hold the handle of the brush so it points straight up toward the ceiling. Slowly paint the curlicues, allowing the paint to flow from the brush.

Continued on page 73

Pears & Grapes Worksheet

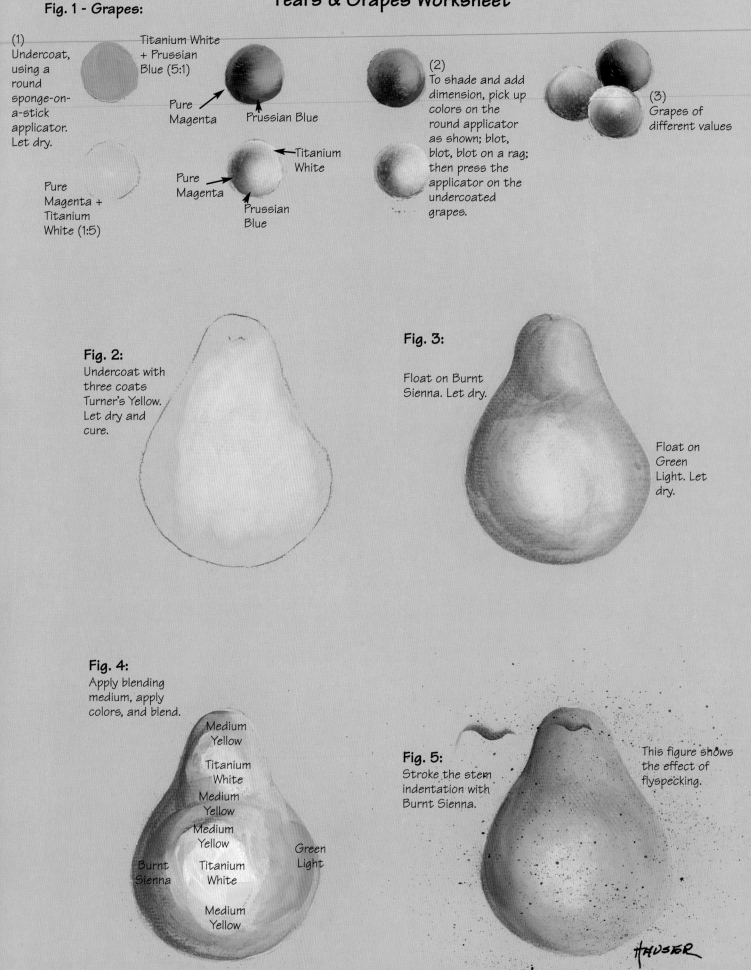

Fig. 1 - Grapes:

(1) Undercoat, using a round sponge-on-a-stick applicator. Let dry.

Titanium White + Prussian Blue (5:1)

Pure Magenta

Prussian Blue

Pure Magenta + Titanium White (1:5)

Titanium White

Pure Magenta

Prussian Blue

(2) To shade and add dimension, pick up colors on the round applicator as shown; blot, blot, blot on a rag; then press the applicator on the undercoated grapes.

(3) Grapes of different values

Fig. 2:

Undercoat with three coats Turner's Yellow. Let dry and cure.

Fig. 3:

Float on Burnt Sienna. Let dry.

Float on Green Light. Let dry.

Fig. 4:

Apply blending medium, apply colors, and blend.

Medium Yellow

Titanium White

Medium Yellow

Medium Yellow

Burnt Sienna

Titanium White

Green Light

Medium Yellow

Fig. 5:

Stroke the stem indentation with Burnt Sienna.

This figure shows the effect of flyspecking.

HAUSER

72

Pears & Grapes Worksheet

Fig. 6:
Undercoat stem with light brown mix
(Burnt Umber + Titanium White, 1:4)

Fig. 7:
Apply blending medium and
reapply light brown mix.

Highlight with
Titanium White.

Titanium
White

Burnt
Umber

Shade with
Burnt Umber.

Fig. 8:
Pull light across.

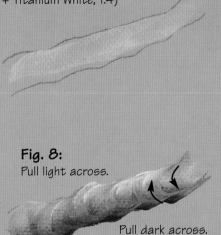

Pull dark across.

Use a light touch.

continued from page 70

worksheet, Fig. 5.

FINISH

Optional Flyspecking:
Fill an old toothbrush with thinned Green Dark (or
other color or colors). Pull your thumb over the bristles
to throw specks (large and small dots) on your surface.
Apply as much or as little as you desire. See the

Varnishing:
1. Apply three or more coats of varnish. Let dry.
2. Rub with a piece of brown paper bag with no printing
   on it to smooth the surface of the wood. Wipe with a
   tack cloth.
3. Apply a final coat of varnish and let dry. ❑

Pattern for Pears & Grapes Shelf Unit
(Actual Size)

Section A

Join sections at
dotted lines for
complete pattern.

A

A

A

A

Section B

Join sections at
dotted lines for
complete pattern.

continued on next page

B

B

Patterns for Pears & Grapes Shelf Unit
(Actual Size)

B

B

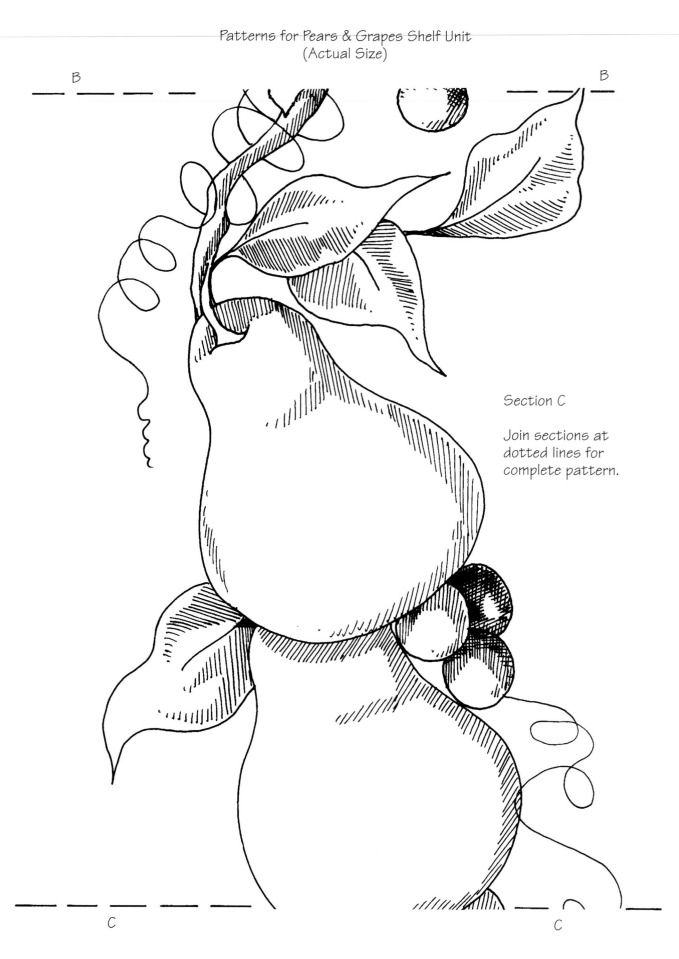

Section C

Join sections at
dotted lines for
complete pattern.

C

C

Patterns for Pears & Grapes Shelf Unit
(Actual Size)

C

C

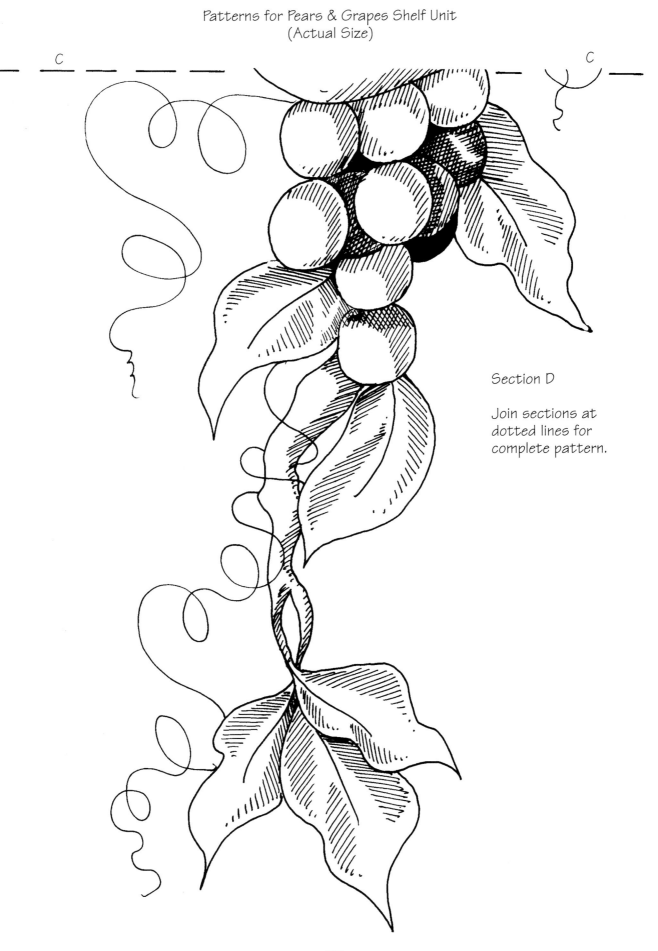

Section D

Join sections at
dotted lines for
complete pattern.

Fly Fishing

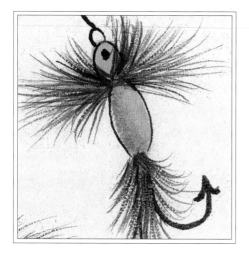

Stool

This stool is a wonderful gift for anyone who enjoys fly fishing. The fishing line and flies make just the right trim detail.

When I found the stool, it was painted white and distressed, so I left it as it was. If you have a new stool, see the "Preparing Your Project" section for how to make new furniture look old.

PALETTE OF COLORS

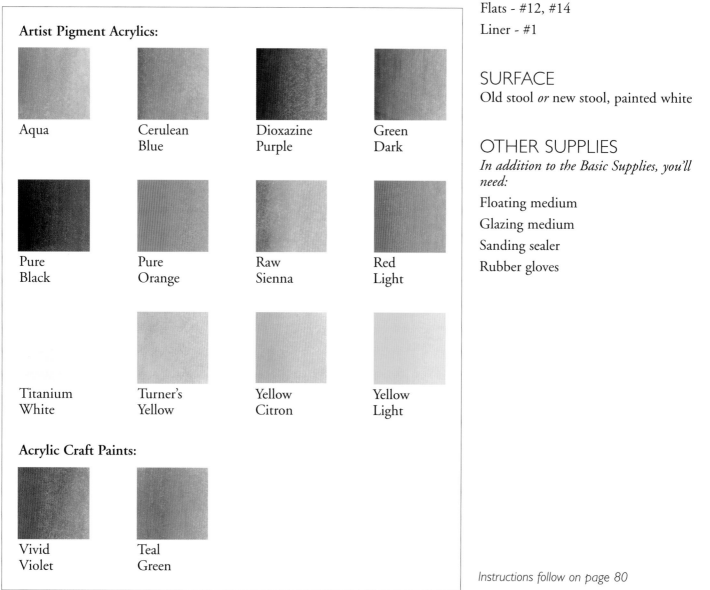

Artist Pigment Acrylics:

Aqua	Cerulean Blue	Dioxazine Purple	Green Dark
Pure Black	Pure Orange	Raw Sienna	Red Light
Titanium White	Turner's Yellow	Yellow Citron	Yellow Light

Acrylic Craft Paints:

Vivid Violet	Teal Green

BRUSHES
Flats - #12, #14
Liner - #1

SURFACE
Old stool *or* new stool, painted white

OTHER SUPPLIES
In addition to the Basic Supplies, you'll need:

Floating medium

Glazing medium

Sanding sealer

Rubber gloves

Instructions follow on page 80

continued from opage 78

PREPARATION

1. Sand the surface lightly. Wipe with a tack cloth.
2. Wipe the surface with a sanding sealer. Let dry. Be sure to wear rubber gloves and follow the manufacturer's instructions.
3. Using water or glazing medium and very little paint, wash colors of your choice from the palette on the top of the stool. Let dry thoroughly.
4. Transfer the pattern, using gray graphite and a stylus.

PAINTING THE DESIGN

See the Fish & Flies Worksheet. The figure numbers refer to those on the worksheet.

Washing Colors on the Fish:

Use very little paint and keep the fish wet with glazing medium or water while you apply colors. See Fig. 1.

1. Using a #14 flat brush, apply water or glazing medium to the fish.
2. Float Green Dark on the top portion of the fish, using very little paint.
3. Wash the area below that with Teal Green + Cerulean Blue.
4. Wash an area below the green with a mix of Dioxazine Purple + Vivid Violet (purple mix).
5. Float an area of Turner's Yellow below the purple area.
6. Finish with a float of Red Light + the purple mix on the belly of the fish and on the fins. Let dry thoroughly.

Add more color to deepen.

1. Repeat steps 1 through 6 to deepen colors. Apply the washes very lightly. Let dry between each wash. (Fig. 2)
2. Apply a wash of Aqua to fins. (Fig. 2)
3. Merge colors so they look like a rainbow. Add some of the colors to the fins. Continue until you reach the depth of color you want. (Fig. 3)

Fish Details:

See Fig. 4.

1. Paint Turner's Yellow circles and half-circles on the top area of the fish using a #1 liner brush.
2. On the side of the fish, stipple lightly with Dioxazine Purple and add touches of Cerulean Blue.
3. Transfer the face pattern to the fish.
4. Float Titanium White on the gills and mouth. Repeat if necessary.
5. Float around the gills with Cerulean Blue.
6. Paint the mouth with a wash of Red Light.
7. Using a liner brush filled with Titanium White, place a spiral stroke for the eye.

See Fig. 5.

1. Paint the eye with Titanium White, Pure Black, and floats of Cerulean Blue.
2. Outline the eye with Pure Black.
3. Redefine the gills with Titanium White. Shade with Cerulean Blue.

Flies & Fishing Line Trim:

See Fig. 6 for examples.

1. Paint the bodies of the flies with colors from the palette, using a #12 flat brush.
2. Using a #1 liner and thinned paint, pull the feather strokes with any of the colors from the palette.
3. Paint the "eyes" on the flies with Pure Black.
4. Outline the bodies of the flies and paint the hooks and line using the #1 liner brush with thinned Pure Black. Let dry thoroughly.

FINISH

1. Apply three or more coats of varnish. Let dry.
2. Rub with a piece of brown paper bag with no printing on it to smooth the surface of the wood. Wipe with a tack cloth.
3. Apply a final coat of varnish and let dry. ❑

Fish & Flies Worksheet

Fig. 1:
Wet with water or glazing medium and wash
on these colors:

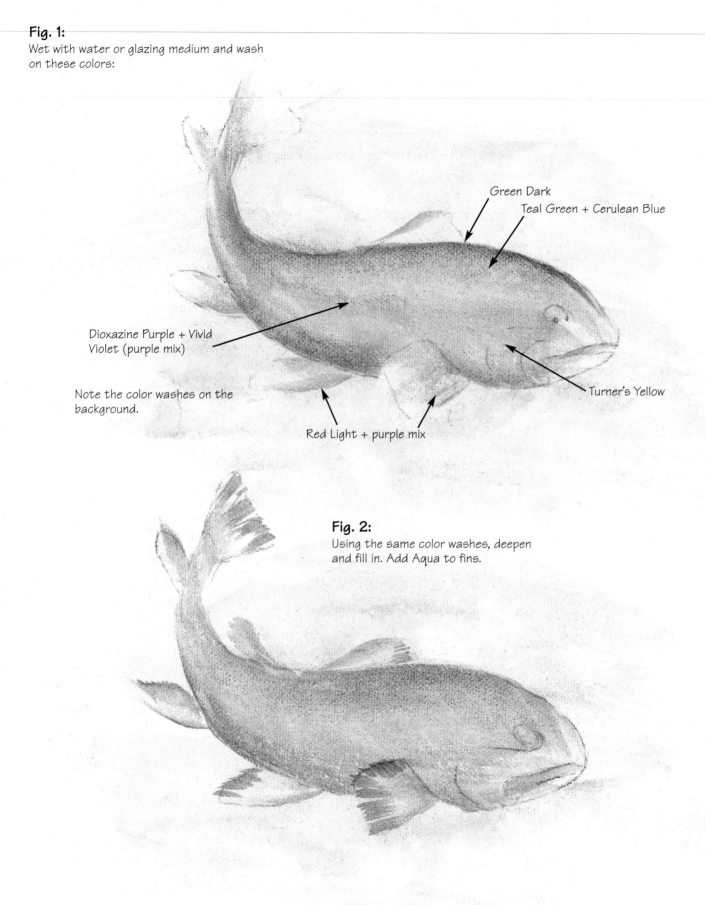

Green Dark

Teal Green + Cerulean Blue

Dioxazine Purple + Vivid
Violet (purple mix)

Note the color washes on the
background.

Red Light + purple mix

Turner's Yellow

Fig. 2:
Using the same color washes, deepen
and fill in. Add Aqua to fins.

Fish & Flies Worksheet

Fig. 3:
Deepen colors even more. Fill in and merge colors so they look like a rainbow. Add some of the colors to the fins.

Fig. 4:
Paint linework with Turner's Yellow.

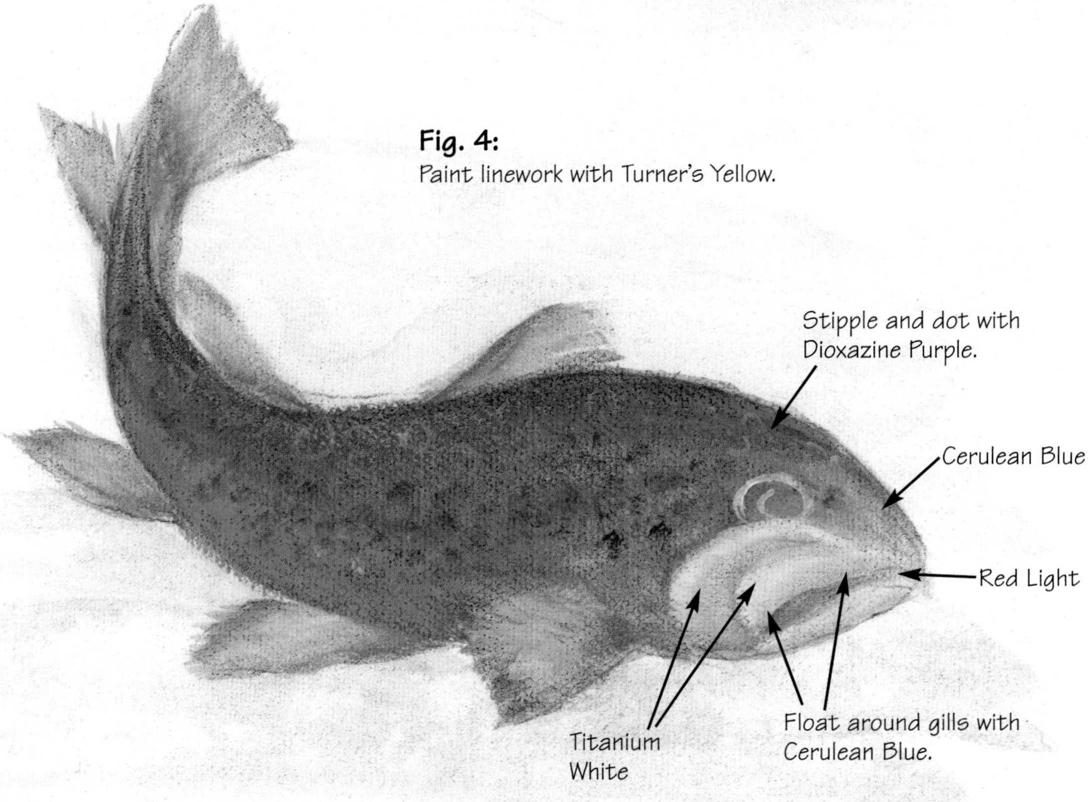

Stipple and dot with Dioxazine Purple.

Cerulean Blue

Red Light

Titanium White

Float around gills with Cerulean Blue.

Fish & Flies Worksheet

Fig. 5:

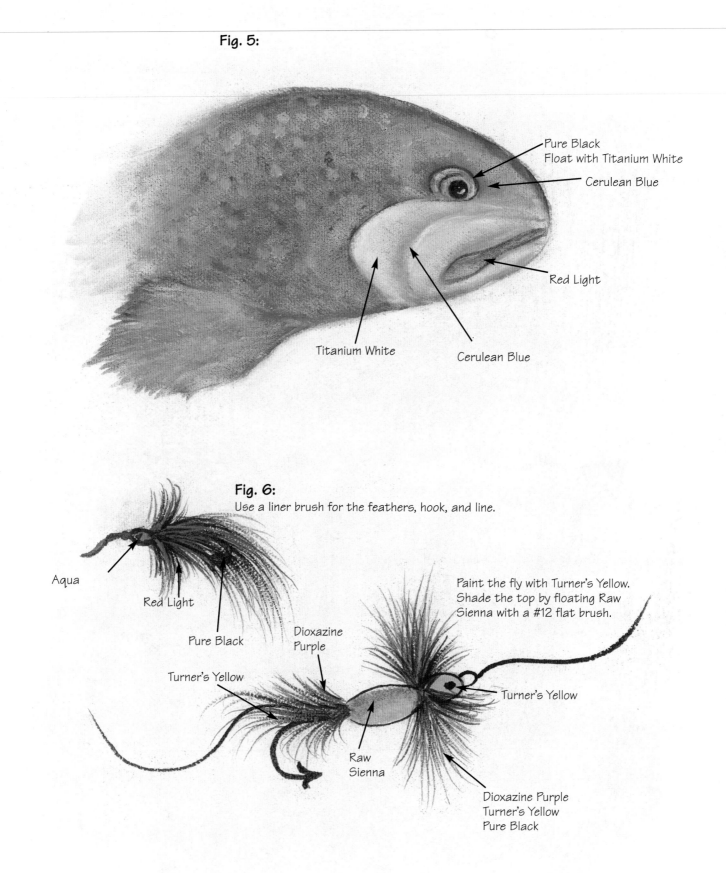

Pure Black
Float with Titanium White

Cerulean Blue

Red Light

Titanium White

Cerulean Blue

Fig. 6:
Use a liner brush for the feathers, hook, and line.

Aqua

Red Light

Pure Black

Turner's Yellow

Dioxazine
Purple

Raw
Sienna

Paint the fly with Turner's Yellow.
Shade the top by floating Raw
Sienna with a #12 flat brush.

Turner's Yellow

Dioxazine Purple
Turner's Yellow
Pure Black

Pattern for Fly Fishing Stool
Enlarge @150% for actual size.

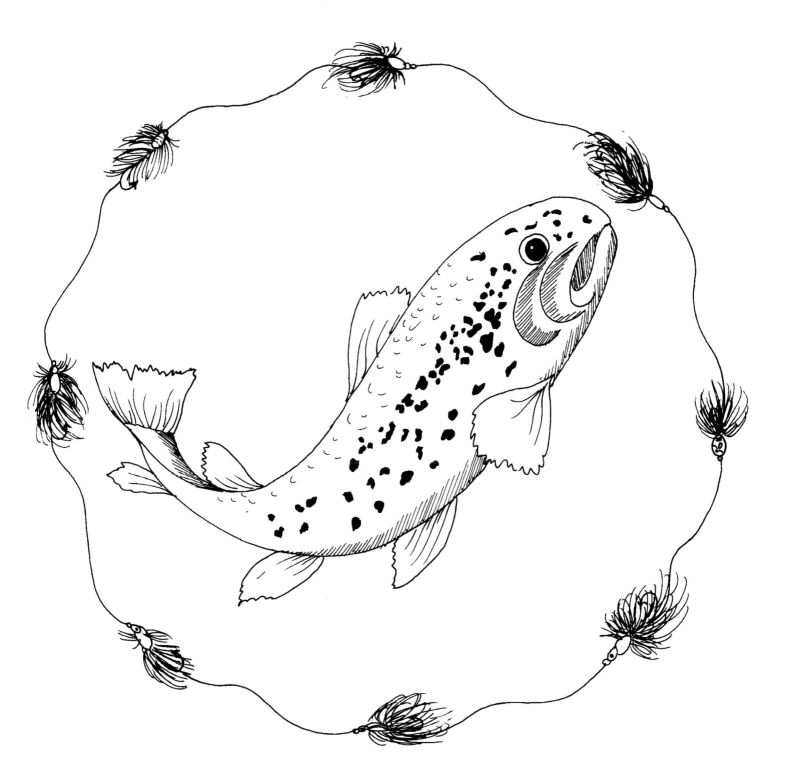

Polka Dots & Tulips

Cabinet

This wonderful little cabinet was painted white when I found it. Because I thought it was charming as it was, preparation was minimal. Painting the dots was easy with a sponge-on-a-stick applicator.

PALETTE OF COLORS

Artist Pigment Acrylics:

Burnt Carmine

Green Dark

Green Light

Green Medium

Green Umber

Ice Green Light

Naphthol Crimson

Prussian Blue

Pure Orange

Red Light

Titanium White

True Burgundy

Acrylic Craft Paints:

Apple Spice

Bright Green

BRUSHES

Flats - #4, #8, #12, #16, #20

Liner - #1

SURFACE

White-painted cabinet

OTHER SUPPLIES

In addition to the Basic Supplies, you'll need:

Blending medium

Liquid sandpaper

Painter's tape or clear cellophane tape

Sponge-on-a-stick applicators, 1/4" diameter

Rubber gloves

Instructions follow on page 88

continued from page 86

PREPARATION

1. Lightly sand the chest as needed. Wipe with a tack cloth.
2. Wipe with a liquid sanding preparation and let dry thoroughly. Be sure to wear rubber gloves and follow the manufacturer's directions.

Polka Dot Border:

1. Using tape, mask off the red borders, 1/2", using the photo as a guide.
2. Apply three or more coats of Apple Spice to the borders, letting the paint dry between coats. Remove tape.
3. Using a pencil, draw a line 1" from the inside edge of the red borders. This is the area where dots will be placed.
4. Using the photo as a guide, mark the placement of the dots with a pencil, creating a staggered pattern.
5. Fill the round sponge-on-a-stick applicator with Apple Spice. Blot on a rag. Press the applicator to the surface to make the dots. A second and, possibly, third coat may be needed for solid coverage. Let dry.
6. Paint a narrow border along the drawn pencil line using a liner brush filled with Bright Green. A second and perhaps a third coat may be needed to cover.

PAINTING THE DESIGN

See the Tulips Worksheet. The figure numbers refer to those on the worksheet.

Tulip Leaves & Stems:

1. Neatly undercoat the leaves and stems with two or three coats of Bright Green. (Fig. 1) Let dry between applications. Let dry and cure.
2. Make a deep green mix (Green Umber + Prussian Blue, 4:1). Double load a large flat brush with water and the green mixture. Float your shadows. (Fig. 1) Let dry and cure. A second or third coat may be applied

to deepen the shadows. Let dry.

3. Working one leaf at a time, beginning at the back and working forward, apply blending medium to the leaf. Apply the colors shown on the worksheet. (Fig. 2) Wipe the brush and blend from the bottom upward and from the top back down. Use a light touch. If the paint feels like it is drying, add a little more blending medium and paint. *Tip:* Use lots of paint when blending acrylics.
4. Paint the stems with Green light. Shade with Green Dark. Highlight with Ice Green Light. (Fig. 2)
5. Add floats of Green Dark to the shadows to brighten the leaves.

Tulips:

1. Undercoat the tulips with two or more coats of Apple Spice. (Fig. 1) Let dry and cure.
2. Neatly transfer the outlines of individual petals to the undercoated areas.
3. Mix a shadow color (True Burgundy + Burnt Carmine, 3:1). Double load a large flat brush with water and the shadow color. Neatly float all the shadows. (Fig. 1) Let dry.
4. Working one petal at a time, beginning with the back petals, apply a small amount of blending medium. Apply the colors shown on the worksheet. Blend, using a light touch. (Fig. 2) Paint the front petal last. (Fig. 3)
5. When the tulips are dry, wash over them with orange or yellow. (Fig. 4) Let dry and cure.

FINISH

1. Apply three or more coats of varnish. Let dry.
2. Rub with a piece of brown paper bag with no printing on it to smooth the surface of the wood.
3. Apply a final coat of varnish and let dry. ❑

TIPS FOR USING SPONGE-ON-A-STICK APPLICATOR:

- Practice on a brown paper bag before painting on your project.

- Follow these steps:
  1. Dab the applicator in blending medium. Blot on a rag.

  2. Fill with paint. Blot, blot, blot.

  3. Pick up more paint. Blot again.

  4. Press on the surface.

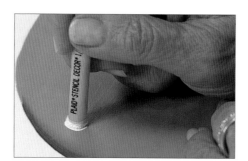

Closeup view of cabinet door

Tulips Worksheet

Fig. 1:
Undercoat with 2-3 coats
Bright Green. Let dry.

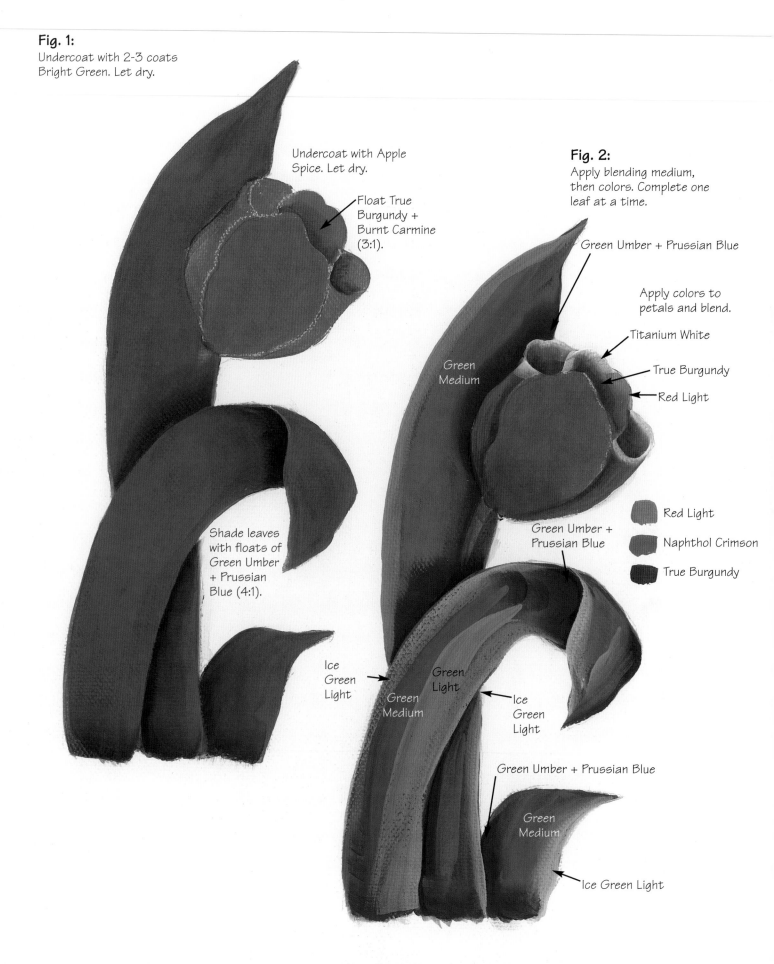

Undercoat with Apple
Spice. Let dry.

Float True
Burgundy +
Burnt Carmine
(3:1).

Fig. 2:
Apply blending medium,
then colors. Complete one
leaf at a time.

Green Umber + Prussian Blue

Apply colors to
petals and blend.

Titanium White

Green
Medium

True Burgundy

Red Light

Shade leaves
with floats of
Green Umber
+ Prussian
Blue (4:1).

Green Umber +
Prussian Blue

Red Light

Naphthol Crimson

True Burgundy

Ice
Green
Light

Green
Light

Green
Medium

Ice
Green
Light

Green Umber + Prussian Blue

Green
Medium

Ice Green Light

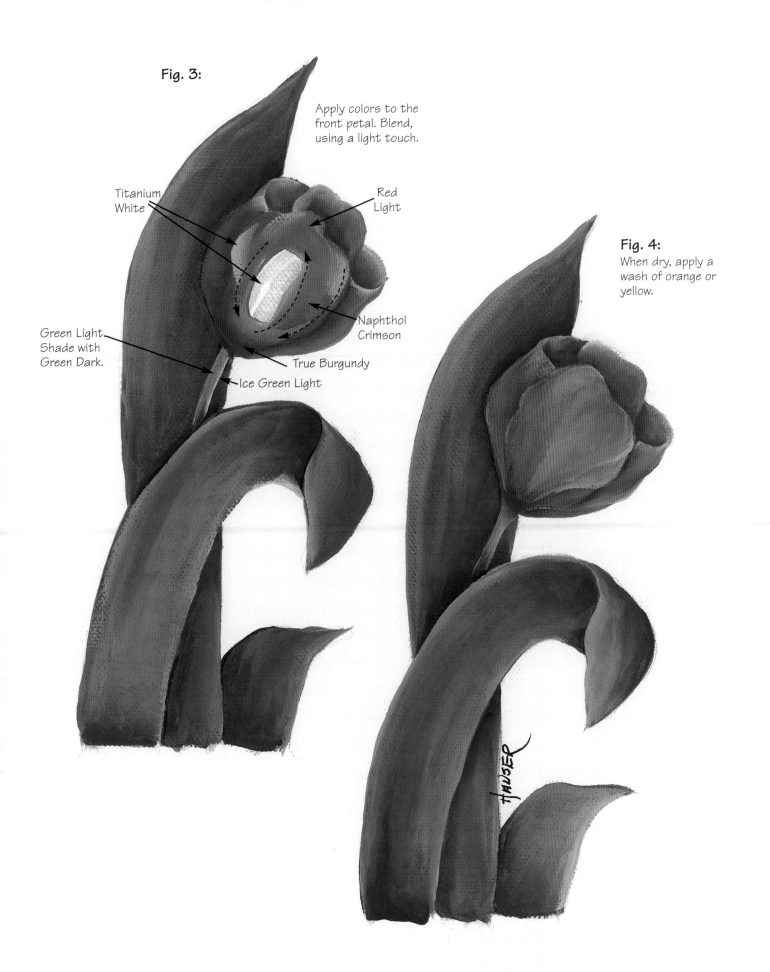

Fig. 3:

Apply colors to the front petal. Blend, using a light touch.

Titanium White

Red Light

Green Light. Shade with Green Dark.

True Burgundy

Ice Green Light

Naphthol Crimson

Fig. 4:
When dry, apply a wash of orange or yellow.

91

Pattern for Polka Dots & Tulips
Bedside Cabinet
Enlarge @140% for actual size.

Spring Flowers

Candle Table &
Captain's Chair

This wonderful little table, which was once called a smoker's table, was in bad shape when I found it. I painted it and decorated it with spring flowers. I chose a coordinated design and colors for an old wooden captain's chair. Don't they make a charming pair?

PALETTE OF COLORS

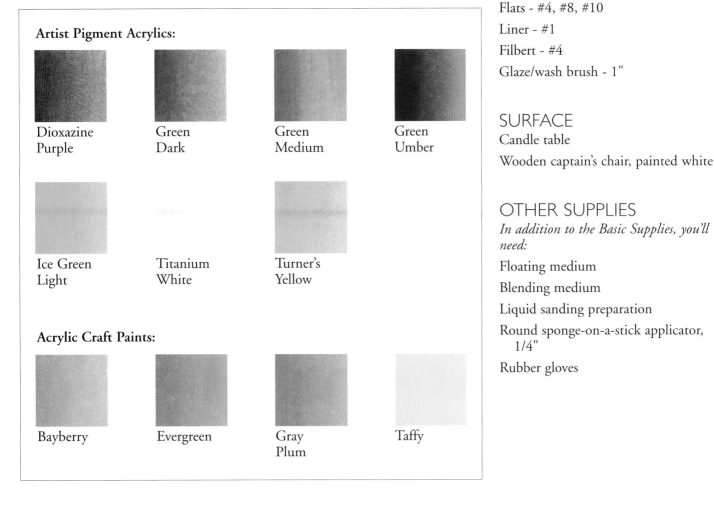

Artist Pigment Acrylics:

Dioxazine Purple

Green Dark

Green Medium

Green Umber

Ice Green Light

Titanium White

Turner's Yellow

Acrylic Craft Paints:

Bayberry

Evergreen

Gray Plum

Taffy

BRUSHES
Flats - #4, #8, #10
Liner - #1
Filbert - #4
Glaze/wash brush - 1"

SURFACE
Candle table
Wooden captain's chair, painted white

OTHER SUPPLIES
In addition to the Basic Supplies, you'll need:
Floating medium
Blending medium
Liquid sanding preparation
Round sponge-on-a-stick applicator, 1/4"
Rubber gloves

PREPARATION

Table:
1. Sand the table. Wipe with a tack cloth.
2. Basecoat with several coats of Bayberry. Let dry thoroughly.
3. Neatly trace and transfer the design, using white graphite paper or chalk.

Chair:
1. Lightly sand the chair, if needed. Wipe with a tack cloth.
2. Basecoat the cushion area of the chair with several coats of Bayberry. Let the paint dry between each coat. Let dry thoroughly after last coat.

Instructions continue on page 96

continued from page 95

3. Choose some trim areas on the legs and back and arm spindles, using the photo as a guide. Paint with Bayberry. Let dry.

4. Double load a #1 flat wash brush with Green Dark and floating medium. Blend on your palette to soften the color so the color graduates through the hairs of the brush from dark to medium to clear. Float this all the way around the inside edge of the cushion area to shade. (**photo 1**) Let dry.

5. Neatly trace and transfer the design to the back of the chair with white graphite paper or chalk.

CREATING THE POLKA DOTS

Using the photos as guides for placement, scatter them throughout the flower designs and on the seat of the chair. See the worksheet for examples.

1. Dip the sponge-on-a-stick applicator in blending medium and blot on a rag, then dip in Taffy and blot on a rag. Press on the surface to apply the larger dots. (**photo 2**)

2. For the smaller dots, use the handle end of a paint brush. Dip in Taffy that has been thinned with water. (**photo 3**)

PAINTING THE DESIGN

See the Spring Flowers Worksheet. The figure numbers refer to those on the worksheet

Leaves:

See Fig. 6 on worksheet.

1. Undercoat with two or more coats of Evergreen. Let dry between coats. Dry thoroughly.

2. Float shadows at the base of the leaves with a shading mix (Green Umber + Dioxazine Purple, 3:1). Let dry.

3. Apply a small amount of blending medium. Apply the shading mix at the base, Green Medium in the middle, and Ice Green Light on the top. Wipe the brush and blend. *Tip:* These leaves require very little paint for blending.

Flowers:

1. Undercoat the flowers with two or more coats of Gray Plum. Let dry. (Figs. 1 and 2.)

2. Double load the brush with floating medium and Dioxazine Purple. Blend on the palette to soften the color so the color graduates through the hairs of the brush from dark to medium to clear. Float this color at the base of each petal. Blend just slightly and lightly. (Fig. 3)

3. Paint the centers of the flowers with the liner brush and tiny dots of very thin, ink-like Titanium White. (Fig. 4)

4. Apply a dot of thinned Turner's Yellow in the center. (Fig. 5)

Continued on page 98

CHAIR SEAT

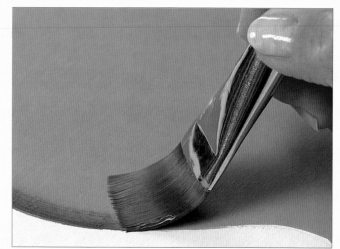

Photo 1 - Floating shading around the edges of the chair "cushion"

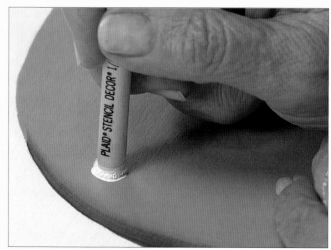

Photo 2 - Making the large dots with a sponge-on-a-stick applicator

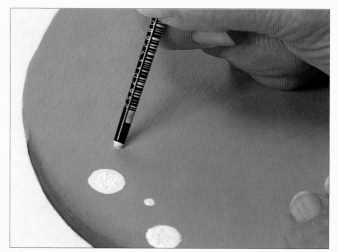

Photo 3 - Making small dots with the handle end of a paint brush

Closeup view of chair back

continued from page 96

Stems & Curlicues:
1. Paint stems with Evergreen.
2. Shade with Green Umber + Dioxazine Purple (3:1).
3. Use the shading mix to paint the curlicues.

Border Leaves:
1. Paint the vines, using a liner brush filled with Green Umber + Dioxazine Purple (3:1) thinned with water to an ink-like consistency.
2. Paint the little leaves, using the filbert brush double loaded with Green Medium and Green Umber.

FINISHING
1. Apply three or more coats of varnish. Let dry.
2. Rub with a piece of brown paper bag with no printing on it to smooth the surface of the wood. Wipe with a tack cloth.
3. Apply a final coat of varnish and let dry. ❑

Closeup view of cabinet side.

Spring Flowers Worksheet

Fig. 1:
Stroke petals from outside toward the center with Gray Plum.

Fig. 2:
Paint five petals for each flower.

Fig. 3:
Float Dioxazine Purple at the center of each petal.

Fig. 4:
Add tiny dots of thinned Titanium White.

Fig. 5:
Add a dot of Turner's Yellow.

4. Apply colors.

Ice Green Light

Green Medium

Green Umber + Dioxazine Purple

5. Blend.

Fig. 6:
1. Undercoat with Evergreen. Let dry.
2. Float Green Umber + Dioxazine Purple (3:1). Let dry.
3. Working one leaf at a time, apply blending medium.

Pattern for Spring Flowers Candle Table
Top & Sides
(Sides are painted without flowers)
Enlarge @120% for actual size.

For Chair Back:
Use section of vine with flowers.
Refer to photo for placement.

Pattern for Spring Flowers Cabinet Front
Enlarge @120% for actual size.

Pattern for Legs of Spring
Flowers Candle Stand

Dragonfly & Bamboo

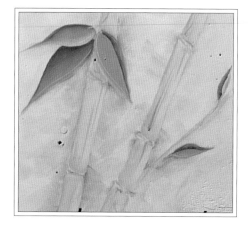

Planter

I found this at a roadside shop. It was painted white with a soft yellow inside and had been used as a plant stand. It could hold all kinds of things, I thought, such as magazines, tools, or towels, as well as potted plants.

I painted the sides with glowing metallic-bodied dragonflies and used a pearlizing medium to paint the wings and framed them with vines and a bamboo border. Bamboo stalks are painted on the ends. Inside, I stenciled some Asian characters to complete the theme.

PALETTE OF COLORS

BRUSHES
Flats - #12, #20

Liner - #1

Filbert - #4

Round - #3

SURFACE
Old plant stand or new unfinished one, painted white

OTHER SUPPLIES
In addition to the Basic Supplies, you'll need:

Pearlizing medium

Glazing medium

Floating medium

Sponge-on-a-stick applicators, 1/4", 5/8"

Stencil with Asian characters

Stencil tape

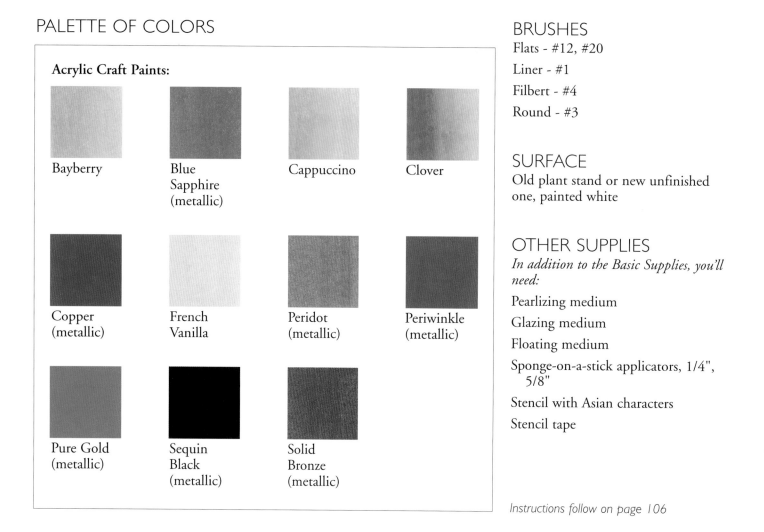

Acrylic Craft Paints:

Bayberry

Blue Sapphire (metallic)

Cappuccino

Clover

Copper (metallic)

French Vanilla

Peridot (metallic)

Periwinkle (metallic)

Pure Gold (metallic)

Sequin Black (metallic)

Solid Bronze (metallic)

Instructions follow on page 106

PREPARATION
Wash and dry the surface to be painted.

CREATING THE BACKGROUND
Work one area at a time.
1. Brush an area with glazing medium. (**photo 1**)
2. Load a #20 flat brush with glazing medium. Pick up a mixture of Bayberry and French Vanilla (1:1) and apply in a slip-slap fashion over the area. (**photo 2**) As you move upward, pick up more glazing medium in your brush to lighten the color.
3. Repeat this procedure with Bayberry, concentrating the color in the areas where the motifs will be painted. Let dry completely.
4. Trace and transfer the design, using the photo as a guide for placement.

PAINTING THE DESIGN
See the Bamboo & Dragonfly Worksheet. The figure numbers refer to those on the worksheets.
Grasses:
1. Undercoat with Bayberry. (Fig. 12)
2. Using a #4 filbert brush, shade with Clover. (Fig. 13)
3. Highlight with French Vanilla. (Fig. 14)

Bamboo Stalks:
1. Undercoat with French Vanilla. (Fig. 4)
2. Using a #12 flat brush, apply shading with Cappuccino. (Fig. 4)
3. With a #3 round brush, apply Cappuccino to indicate the sections of the bamboo. (Fig. 4)
4. Using Bayberry, reinforce section divisions and add dimension. (Fig. 5)
5. Repeat, using Clover and covering less area. (Fig. 6)

Bamboo Leaves:
1. Undercoat with Bayberry. (Fig. 1)
2. Using a #4 filbert brush, shade with Clover. (Fig. 2)
3. Highlight and add lines with French Vanilla. (Fig. 3)

Green Dragonfly Bodies:
1. Fill the 1/4" round sponge-on-a-stick applicator with Peridot. (**photo 3**) Blot on a rag. Press on the surface to create the circles that form the dragonfly's body. (Fig. 7) Let dry.
2. Without cleaning the applicator, load one side with Copper. (**photo 4**) Press over the Peridot circles to highlight. (Fig. 8) (**photo 5**) Let dry.

Continued on page 108

Lettering inside planter

CREATING THE BACKGROUND

Photo 1 - Brushing the background with glazing medium.

Photo 2 - Applying color to the background.

PAINTING THE DRAGONFLIES

Photo 3 - Loading a sponge-on-a-stick applicator with paint.

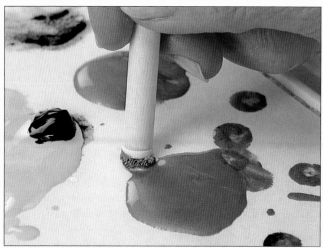

Photo 4 - Loading the side of the applicator with Copper

Photo 5 - Pressing the applicator on the surface.

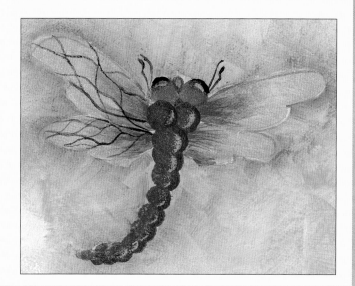

continued from page 106

3. Without cleaning the applicator, add a second highlight by dipping one edge in pearlizing medium. Press over the Copper highlights. (Fig. 9) Let dry.

Bronze Body Dragonflies:
See Fig. 10.
1. Fill the 1/4" round sponge-on-a-stick applicator with Solid Bronze. Blot on rag. Press on the surface to create the circles that form the dragonfly's body. Let dry.
2. Without cleaning the applicator, load one side with Peridot. Press over the Solid Bronze circles. Let dry.
3. Without cleaning the applicator, add a highlight by dipping one edge in pearlizing medium. Press over the Peridot.

Gold Dragonfly Bodies:
See Fig. 11.
1. Fill the 1/4" round sponge-on-a-stick applicator with Pure Gold. Blot on rag. Press on the surface to create the circles that form the dragonfly's body. Let dry.
2. Without cleaning the applicator, load one side with Peridot. Press over the Pure Gold circles. Let dry.
3. Without cleaning the applicator, add a highlight by dipping one edge in pearlizing medium. Press over the Peridot.

Dragonflies' Eyes:
1. Fill the 1/4" round sponge-on-a-stick applicator with Periwinkle. Blot on a rag and press on the surface to paint the eyes. Let dry. (Fig. 7)
2. Add a dot between them with Solid Bronze. (Fig. 7)
3. Using a #1 liner brush, shade with a stroke of thinned Sequin Black. (Fig. 8)
4. Highlight with a comma stroke of pearlizing medium. (Fig. 9)

Dragonflies' Legs:
Using a #1 liner brush and thinned Sequin Black, paint the legs. (Fig. 9)

Wings:
1. Double load a #20 flat brush with floating medium and pearlizing medium. With pearlizing medium to outside, paint the outer portion of wing. (Fig. 7)
2. Double load the #20 flat brush with floating medium and Periwinkle. Paint the inner portion of wings, floating Periwinkle next to the body. (Fig. 8)
3. Load a #1 liner brush with Sequin Black that has been thinned to the consistency of ink. Lightly outline the wings and paint veins on the wings. (Fig. 9) Let dry.
4. Double load a #20 flat brush with Blue Sapphire and floating medium. Float color on the wings to strengthen. (Fig. 9)

Vine:
See Fig. 15.
1. Using a #1 liner brush filled with Cappuccino that has been thinned to the consistency of ink, paint the stem.
2. Paint the leaves, using a #4 filbert brush double loaded with Bayberry and Clover.

Stenciled Characters:
Position the stencil on the surface and tape in place. Dip the 5/8" sponge-on-a-stick applicator in Clover. Blot on a rag. Dab paint through the openings of the stencil to create the characters. Let dry and cure.

FINISH
1. Apply three or more coats of varnish. Let dry.
2. Rub with a piece of brown paper bag with no printing on it to smooth the surface of the wood. Wipe with a tack cloth.
3. Apply a final coat of varnish and let dry. ❏

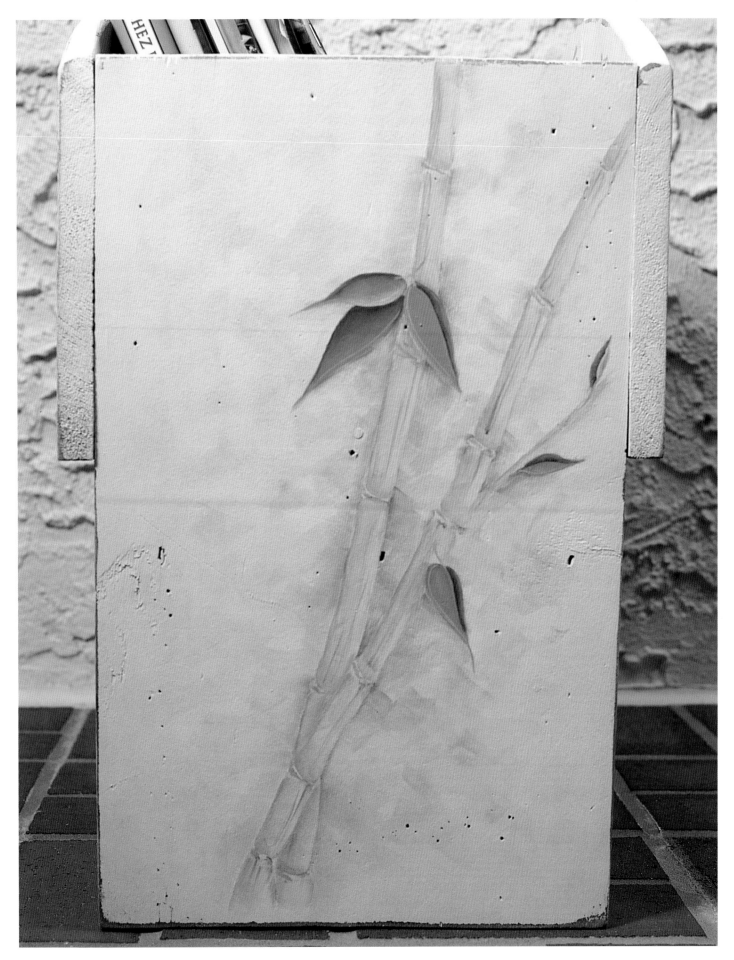

Dragonfly & Bamboo Worksheet

Bamboo

Fig. 1:
Undercoat leaves with Bayberry.

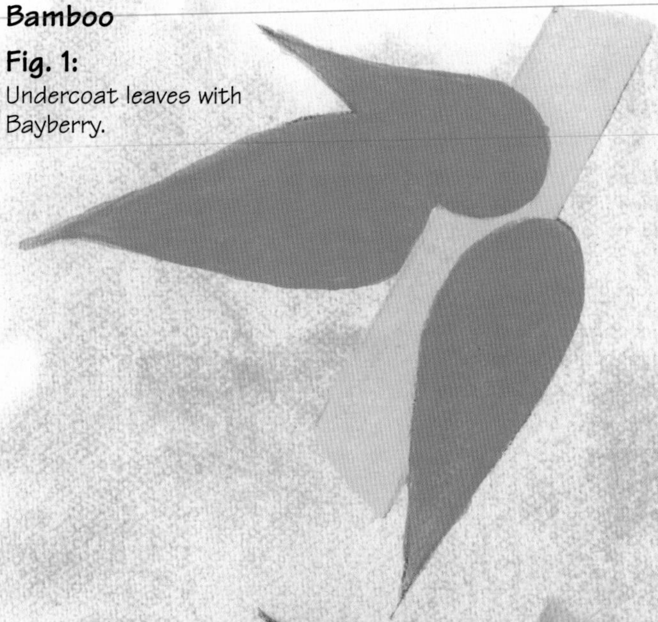

Fig. 4:
Undercoat with French Vanilla.

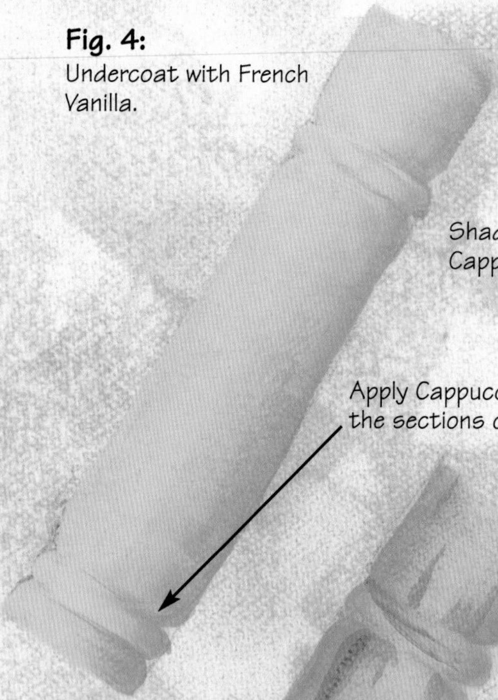

Shade and with Cappuccino.

Apply Cappuccino to indicate the sections of the bamboo.

Fig. 2:
Shade with Clover.

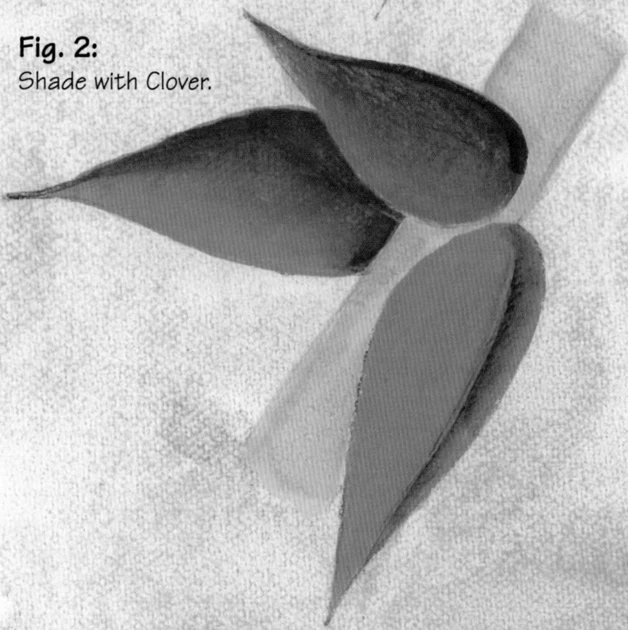

Fig. 5:
With Bayberry, reinforce section divisions and add dimension.

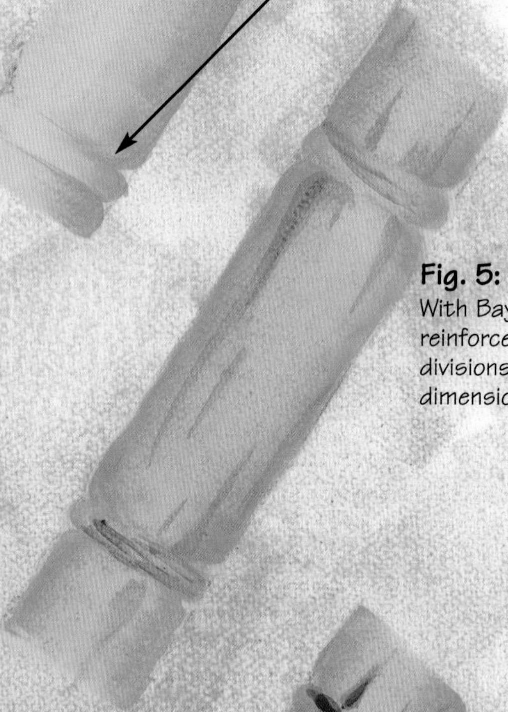

Fig. 3:
Highlight and add lines with French Vanilla.

Fig. 6:
Repeat with Clover, covering less area.

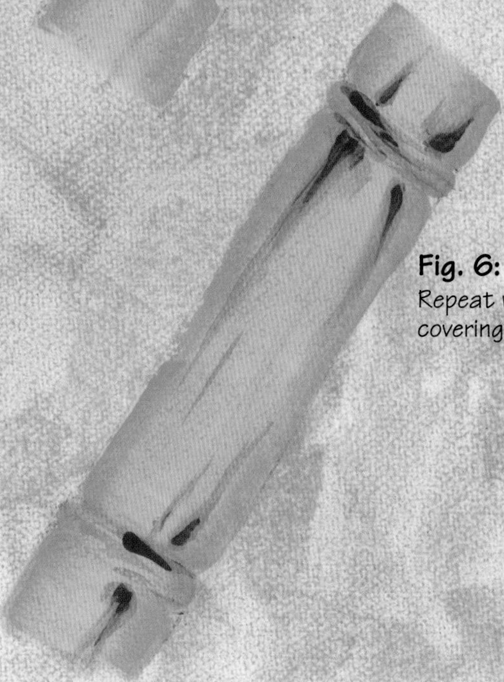

Dragonfly & Bamboo Worksheet

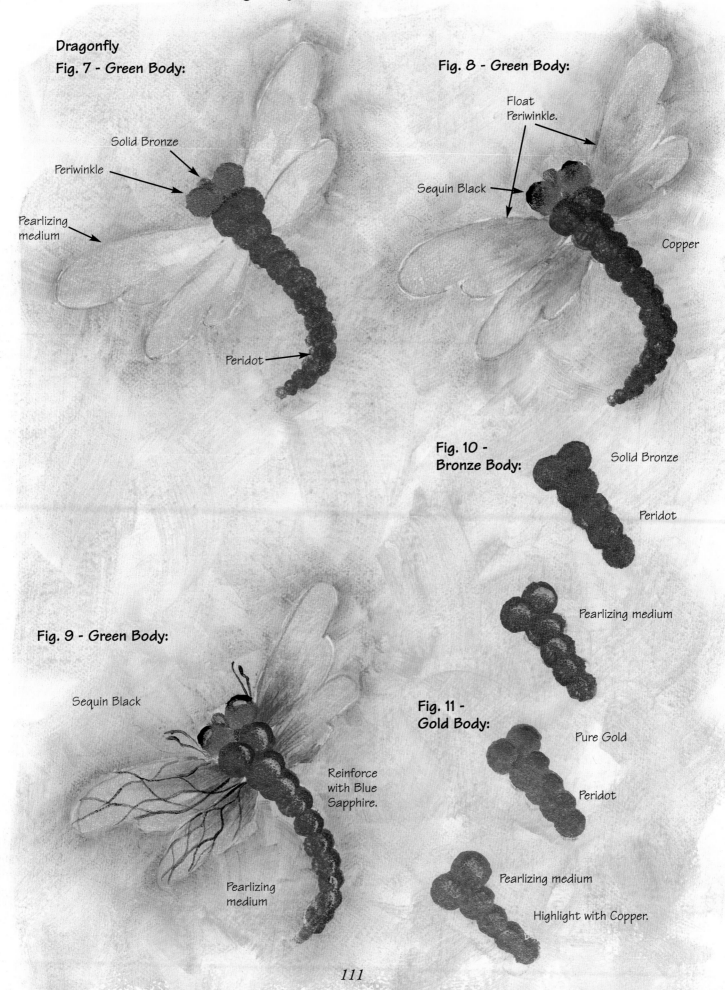

**Dragonfly
Fig. 7 - Green Body:**

Solid Bronze

Periwinkle

Pearlizing medium

Peridot

Fig. 8 - Green Body:

Float Periwinkle.

Sequin Black

Copper

Fig. 10 - Bronze Body:

Solid Bronze

Peridot

Pearlizing medium

Fig. 9 - Green Body:

Sequin Black

Reinforce with Blue Sapphire.

Pearlizing medium

Fig. 11 - Gold Body:

Pure Gold

Peridot

Pearlizing medium

Highlight with Copper.

Dragonfly & Bamboo Worksheet

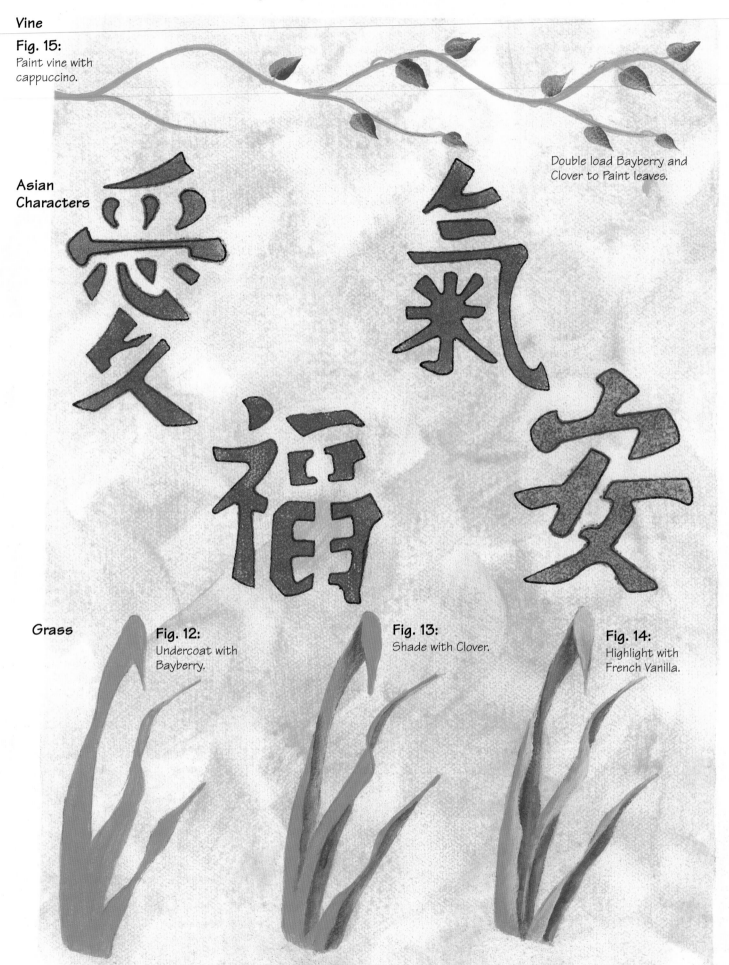

Vine

Fig. 15:
Paint vine with cappuccino.

Double load Bayberry and Clover to Paint leaves.

Asian Characters

Grass

Fig. 12:
Undercoat with Bayberry.

Fig. 13:
Shade with Clover.

Fig. 14:
Highlight with French Vanilla.

Pattern for Sides of Dragonfly Planter
Enlarge @135% for actual size.
Connect at center to complete pattern.

Center Dragonfly
See photo for placement

Pattern for Ends of Dragonfly Planter
Enlarge @ 120% for actual size.
Connect pattern sections to complete.

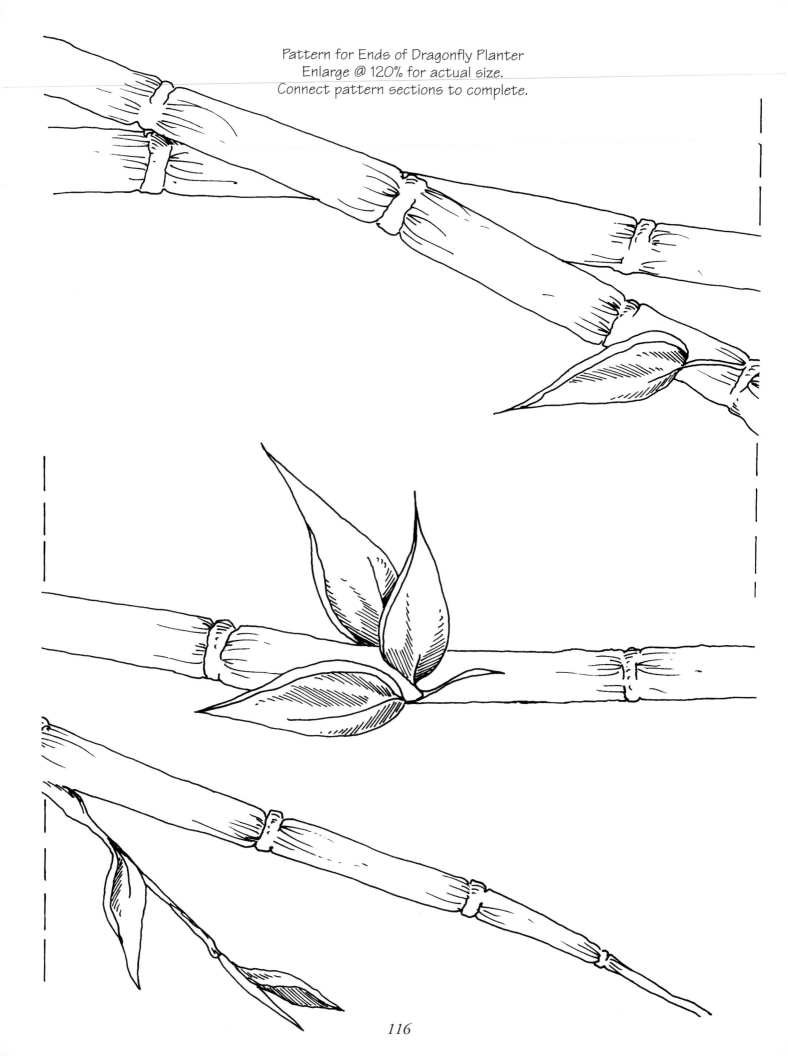

Pattern for Palm Trees Garden Bench
Enlarge @110% for actual size
See instructions on page 118

Palm Trees

Garden Bench

PALETTE OF COLORS

Artist Pigment Acrylics:

Burnt
Sienna

Burnt
Umber

Green
Umber

Ice Green
Light

Turner's
Yellow

Warm
White

Acrylic Craft Paints:

Clover

Country
Twill

Engine
Red

Night
Sky

Wicker
White

This wonderful wooden bench was painted white when I found it, and it needed very little preparation beyond cleaning and sanding. If you have a new bench, paint it white, let dry, and sand for an aged look.

I painted a faux upholstery panel on the bench back and three palm tree "cushions" on the seat. It would be lovely on a porch.

BRUSHES
Flats - #4, #8, #20
Liner - #1
Filbert - #8
Glaze/wash brush - 1"

SURFACE
Old bench

OTHER SUPPLIES
In addition to the Basic Supplies, you'll need:
Blending medium
Glazing medium
Floating medium
Sponge-on-a-stick applicator, 5/8"

PREPARATION
1. Wash and dry the bench.
2. Trace and transfer the pattern.

continued on next page

continued from page 119

PAINTING THE DESIGN

Pillows:

Follow the same procedure for the "cushion" on the bench back and the three seat "cushions."

1. Undercoat each pillow with Ice Green Light.
2. Undercoat the border of each pillow with Country Twill.
3. Double load a #20 flat brush with floating medium and Country Twill. Float Country Twill along the inside edge of the pillow.

Palm Fronds:

See the Palm Trees Worksheet. The figure numbers refer to those on the worksheet.

1. Fill a #1 liner brush with Green Umber. Paint the stalks to establish the shape of the tree.
2. Use the #1 liner with Green Umber to pull lines to create

the fronds. (Fig. 1) Let dry.

3. Use the #1 liner with Clover to pull more lines to make the fronds fuller. (Fig. 2)
4. Use the #1 liner with Night Sky to add a few more. (Fig. 3)

Tree Trunks:

See the Palm Trees Worksheet. Work one tree trunk at a time.

1. Apply blending medium.
2. Double load Burnt Umber and Country Twill on a #8 flat brush. Paint the trunk, placing Burnt Umber on the left side. (Fig. 4)
3. Clean the brush and fully load it with Burnt Umber. Pull modified u-strokes from left to right, using a light touch. (Fig. 5)
4. Clean the brush and fully load it with Country Twill. Pull modified u-strokes from right to left, using a light touch. (Fig. 6)

Continued on page 122

Closeup View of Back Detail

continued from page 120

Ground:

See the Palm Trees Worksheet.

1. Wet the surface with plenty of water. Load a #4 flat with Burnt Umber. Place brush on the wet surface and let the Burnt Umber bleed into the water. (Fig. 4) Let dry fully.
2. Repeat with Green Umber. (Fig. 5) Let dry.

Grasses:

See the Palm Trees Worksheet, Fig. 6.

1. Load a #1 liner with thinned Green Umber and pull long flowing strokes upward.
2. Repeat with Clover, then with Night Sky. Paint fewer strokes with each color added.

Pail:

See the Palm Trees Worksheet.

1. Using a #4 flat brush, undercoat the outside of the pail with Wicker White. Undercoat the inside with Engine Red. (Fig. 13)
2. Paint the stripes and handle using a #1 liner with Engine Red. (Figs. 13 and 14)
3. Paint the rim and the trim on the handle with Wicker White. (Figs. 13 and 15)
4. Place a tiny dot of Wicker White for the handle rivet. (Fig. 15)

Pillow on Back:

See the Palm Trees Worksheet.

1. Load the 5/8" sponge applicator with Country Twill. Press on the surface to make five "buttons." (Fig. 10) Let dry.
2. Double load a 1" wash brush with floating medium and Country Twill. Create a tufted effect around the buttons and float color around the buttons. (Fig. 11) Let dry fully.

3. Double load a #8 filbert with floating medium and Burnt Umber. Float a shadow around the button, working clockwise from 1 o'clock to 7 o'clock. (Fig. 12)
4. Load the 5/8" sponge applicator with Country Twill. Dab the tip in Warm White and blot on the palette to soften the colors. Repaint the button to clean up the edges, locating the Warm White highlight in the upper left. (Fig. 12)

Tassels:

See the Palm Trees Worksheet.

1. Outline the tassel and grommet with thinned Burnt Umber. (Fig. 7)
2. Apply a hit-and-miss wash of Clover. (Fig. 7)
3. Add Burnt Sienna. (Fig. 8)
4. Highlight with Turner's Yellow. (Fig. 9)
5. Paint many fine lines for the tassel threads, using the #1 liner with thinned Burnt Umber. (Fig. 9)

Finishing Touches:

1. Brush glazing medium all around the "pillows." Pick up Burnt Umber and lightly float around the outer edges of all the pillows. Let dry.
2. Repeat with Burnt Umber to reinforce (darken) the right sides of the pillows to create the trompe l'oeil effect.
3. Float Burnt Umber shading on the outer edges of the tassels.
4. Create shadows in the grommets the tassels hang from. See photo on page 121 for reference. Let dry and cure.

FINISH

1. Apply three or more coats of varnish. Let dry.
2. Rub with a piece of brown paper bag with no printing on it to smooth the surface of the wood. Wipe with a tack cloth.
3. Apply a final coat of varnish and let dry. ❏

Palm Trees Worksheet

Fig. 1:
Start with Green Umber.

Fig. 2:
Add Clover.

Fig. 3:
Add a few lines
of Night Sky.

Fig. 4:
Paint trunk with double loaded Burnt Umber and Country Twill, with Burnt Umber on the left.

Wet surface with water. Let Burnt Umber bleed into water.

Fig. 5:
Reinforce trunk with u-strokes of Burnt Umber.

Again wet surface with water. Let Green Umber bleed into water

Fig. 6:
Lighten trunk with u-strokes of Country Twill.

Pull lines of Green Umber, Clover, and Night Sky to paint grass.

Palm Trees Worksheet

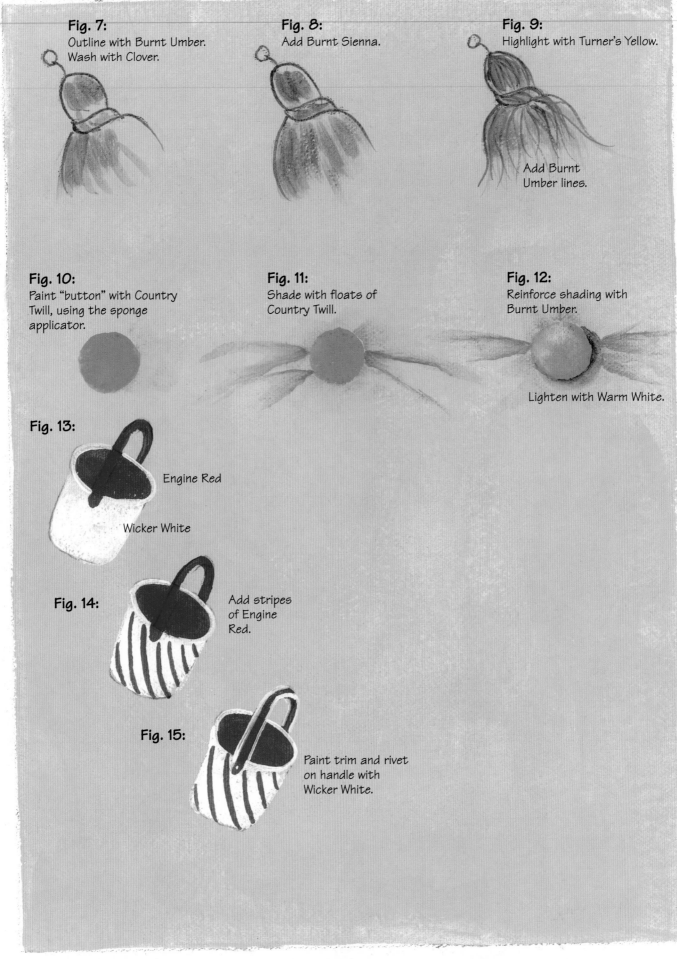

Fig. 7:
Outline with Burnt Umber.
Wash with Clover.

Fig. 8:
Add Burnt Sienna.

Fig. 9:
Highlight with Turner's Yellow.

Add Burnt
Umber lines.

Fig. 10:
Paint "button" with Country
Twill, using the sponge
applicator.

Fig. 11:
Shade with floats of
Country Twill.

Fig. 12:
Reinforce shading with
Burnt Umber.

Lighten with Warm White.

Fig. 13:

Engine Red

Wicker White

Fig. 14:

Add stripes
of Engine
Red.

Fig. 15:

Paint trim and rivet
on handle with
Wicker White.

Metric Conversion Chart

Inches to Millimeters and Centimeters

Inches	MM	CM
1/8	3	.3
1/4	6	.6
3/8	10	1.0
1/2	13	1.3
5/8	16	1.6
3/4	19	1.9
7/8	22	2.2
1	25	2.5
1-1/4	32	3.2
1-1/2	38	3.8
1-3/4	44	4.4
2	51	5.1
3	76	7.6
4	102	10.2
5	127	12.7
6	152	15.2
7	178	17.8
8	203	20.3
9	229	22.9
10	254	25.4
11	279	27.9
12	305	30.5

Yards to Meters

Yards	Meters
1/8	.11
1/4	.23
3/8	.34
1/2	.46
5/8	.57
3/4	.69
7/8	.80
1	.91
2	1.83
3	2.74
4	3.66
5	4.57
6	5.49
7	6.40
8	7.32
9	8.23
10	9.14

Index

Super Paper Airplanes

Biplanes to Space Planes

Norman Schmidt

A Sterling/Tamos Book
Sterling Publishing Co., Inc.   New York

Super
Paper
Airplanes

A Sterling / Tamos Book
© 1995 Norman Schmidt

Sterling Publishing Company, Inc.
387 Park Avenue South, New York, NY 10016

TAMOS Books Inc.
300 Wales Avenue, Winnipeg, MB, Canada R2M 2S9

10   9   8   7   6   5   4   3   2

Distributed in Canada by Sterling Publishing Co., Inc.
c/o Canadian Manda Group, P.O. Box 920, Station U
Toronto, Ontario, Canada M8Z 5P9
Distributed in Great Britain and Europe by Cassell PLC
Villiers House, 41/47 Strand, London WC2N 5JE, England
Distributed in Australia by Capricorn Link (Australia) Pty Ltd.
P.O. Box 6651, Baulkham Hills,
Business Centre, NSW 2153, Australia

Design   Norman Schmidt
Photography   Jerry Grajewski & Walter Kaiser,
               KKS Commercial Photography
Printed in China

CANADIAN CATALOGING IN PUBLICATION DATA

Schmidt, Norman Jacob, 1947-
   Super paper airplanes

   "A Sterling/Tamos book."
   ISBN 1-895569-30-3

1. Paper airplanes.   I. Title.
TL778.S35 1995   745.592   C95-920206-1

LIBRARY OF CONGRESS
CATALOGING IN PUBLICATION DATA

Schmidt, Norman.
   Super paper airplanes : biplanes to space planes / Norman
Schmidt.
       p.   cm.
   "A Sterling/Tamos book."
   Includes index.
   ISBN 1-895569-30-3
   1. Paper airplanes — juvenile literature.
[1. Paper airplanes.]   I. Title
TL778.S364   1995   94-35543
745.592 — dc20   CIP
                                        AC
   ISBN 1-895569-30-3

Contents

The advice and directions given in this book
have been carefully checked, prior to
printing, by the Author as well as the
Publisher. Nevertheless, no guarantee can
be given as to project outcome due to
possible differences in material and the
Author and Publisher will not be
responsible for the results.

Flight

People have been obsessed with the idea of flight ever since they looked into the sky and saw birds soaring gently overhead. Mythical stories in many cultures around the world have flying creatures of all sorts, including human beings. When did the reality of human flight begin?

Archeologists in Egypt have discovered a small wooden bird, carved from lightweight sycamore wood, that has a very aerodynamic shape. This small wooden bird is unlike any real bird because its tail has both horizontal and vertical surfaces, just like present-day airplanes. It is not known whether this was a toy, a weather vane, or a small model of some larger craft.

There are other examples of flying toys, such as the Saqqara bird invented by the Greek philosopher Archytas in about 345 B.C. It was a small wooden dove attached to an arm that allowed it to "lift off" in wavering flight. It is not known how the bird was propelled. At about the same time the Chinese philosopher Mo Tzu constructed what was possibly the first kite, which is simply a tethered airplane. Some Europeans made wings of wood, cloth, and bird feathers, strapped them to their arms, and jumped off high buildings. In 1020 Eilmer "the flying monk" did this, and attained some success with flight, but broke both his legs in the attempt. In the 1500s the artist and inventor, Leonardo da Vinci, made many drawings and models of different kinds of aircraft, including the parachute. Another story from the 1700s tells of a French locksmith named Besnier, who, with wings strapped to his arms and legs, jumped from a tall building and glided over neighboring houses.

The development of kites continued and they became the forerunners of free-flying airplanes. European inventors and scientists used them to carry out experiments in aerodynamic forces. Such experiments led to the first free-flying airplanes of Sir George Cayley in the 1790s. They demonstrated the principles of flight as they are understood today. In the 1850s Sir George's coachman was among the first people to fly in an actual airplane. The stage was now set for the development of controllable airplanes. That story is told through the paper airplanes that follow in this book.

Construction

When carefully made, the paper airplanes in this book are super flyers. They can be built using ordinary 20 or 24 lb bond copier paper measuring 8-1/2 in by 11 in (21.6cm by 27.9cm). Bond paper is lightweight, easy to cut and fold, and easy to fasten together. It is available in a variety of colors (black paper may have to be purchased from an art store). Since a paper airplane's lift and thrust are limited, every effort must be made to keep drag at a minimum. Every surface not parallel to the direction of travel (wings, nose, and canopy) adds drag, so the neater and more accurate your construction, the better the plane will fly. Clean and accurate cuts and crisp folds are a top priority.

Measuring and Cutting Use a sharp pencil to mark the measurements and draw firm, accurate lines. Cut out the pieces with a sharp pair of scissors or a craft knife and a steel-edged ruler. A knife makes a cleaner cut. When using a knife be sure to work on a proper cutting surface.

Folding Always lay the paper on a level surface for folding. Folding is easier along a score line (an indented line on the paper made with a hard pencil drawn along a ruler). There are only three kinds of folds used in making the airplanes in this book. They are mountain folds, valley folds, and sink folds. Where multiple layers are folded, run your fingers back and forth along the fold pressing hard to make a sharp crease.

Gluing A glue stick works well for paper airplanes. Follow the instructions for gluing. Cover the entire contacting surfaces that are to be joined. If there are multiple layers, apply glue to each of the sheets. Glue should be used sparingly, but use enough to hold the parts together. Where multiple layers are being joined you may need to hold the pieces for a few minutes until the glue sets.

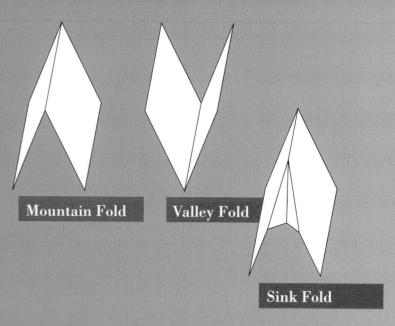

Mountain Fold   Valley Fold

Sink Fold

A mountain fold and a valley fold are actually the same kind of fold. Both are made by folding a flat piece of paper and sharply creasing the fold line. The only difference is that one folds up (valley fold) and the other folds down (mountain fold). They are distinguished only for convenience in giving instructions.

To make a sink fold, begin with paper that has been folded using a mountain (or valley) fold and measure as required across the folded corner. Then push in the corner along the measured lines, making a diagonal fold. Finish by creasing the folds sharply.

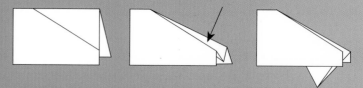

Trimming for Flight

Air is made up of small, solid, evenly spaced particles called molecules. Everything in the universe is made up of molecules, but air molecules are quite far apart compared to those that make up metal, wood, or paper, and they are easily separated when a body moves through them. The molecules are piled up in a thick layer from the ground, and this is called the atmosphere. It forms part of the space around us and the sky above us. This layer of air molecules (atmosphere) exerts pressure on everything in the world and it is this pressure that makes flight possible. The shape of the airplane affects the molecules as they move across the airplane's surfaces, increasing or decreasing air pressure, determining the flight characteristics of the plane.

No paper airplanes are perfectly straight. And they are easily bent. Shown right below is an example of trimming using the rudder. Airplane A flies straight because air flows smoothly along its surfaces. It needs no trim. Airplane B yaws to the left because the air on the left is deflected by the bent fuselage, increasing air pressure on that side. The rudder is used to compensate. Airplane C again flies straight because it has been trimmed so that the deflected air on the left is opposed by air being deflected by the rudder on the right. But airplane C does not fly as well as airplane A because it is creating much more drag.

Before making any trim adjustments to a paper airplane that you have just constructed, be sure you are releasing the plane correctly for flight. Always begin with a gentle straight-ahead release, keeping the wings level. Hold the plane between thumb and forefinger just behind the center of gravity. As your technique improves you can throw harder, adjusting the trim as needed. But remember, all planes do not fly at the same speed.

NOTE: Fly Safely. Some of the airplanes in this book have sharp points so never fly them toward another person. If you fly the airplanes outdoors they may go farther than you expect. Be sure they do not go into the street where you will have to retrieve them.

AIRPLANE CONTROL SURFACES

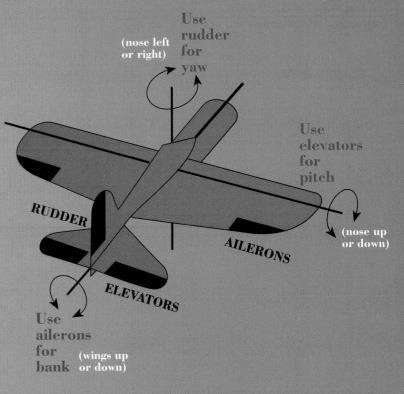

(nose left or right) Use rudder for yaw

Use elevators for pitch

(nose up or down)

RUDDER

AILERONS

ELEVATORS

Use ailerons for bank (wings up or down)

HOW TRIMMING WORKS

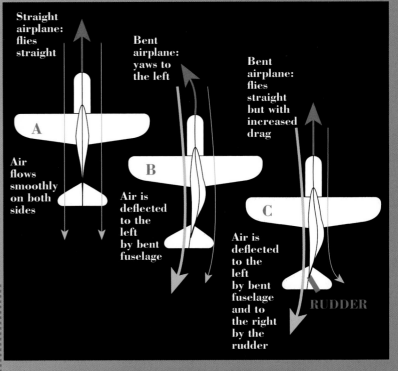

Straight airplane: flies straight

Bent airplane: yaws to the left

Bent airplane: flies straight but with increased drag

A

Air flows smoothly on both sides

B

Air is deflected to the left by bent fuselage

C

Air is deflected to the left by bent fuselage and to the right by the rudder

RUDDER

Aero Bat

HISTORICAL INFORMATION

The earliest aircraft designers looked to birds and bats for clues about airplane construction. They built them with thin wooden frames cross-braced with wires and covered in fabric. For control while in flight, the wing tips could be bent up or down as necessary by the pilot. But the airplanes were flimsy and difficult to fly. They often fluttered badly and some collapsed. Many crashed. Between the 1790s and the 1890s Sir George Cayley, Francis Wenham, Percy Pilcher, Lawrence Hargrave, Otto Lilienthal, and others, experimented with various bird-like airplane designs. This paper airplane is modeled on early bird-like planes.

Technical Information

Lift When a wing having a curved upper surface moves forward it slices the air into two layers – one above and one beneath the wing. Both air layers are made up of the same number of molecules, but those that move over the curved top of the wing have farther to go. So they must speed up and spread farther apart which causes them to exert less downward pressure. The molecules of air beneath the wing remain more closely spaced buoying up the airplane. Raising the leading edge of the wing slightly (the angle of attack), increases the difference in pressure above and below the wing, adding more buoyancy.

Gravity This force pulls everything in the world to the ground and opposes lift. Therefore an airplane's center of gravity (the point at which an object balances) must coincide with the lift created by the wings. If it doesn't the airplane is unstable. With the center of gravity too far back the nose will pitch up; too far forward and the nose will pitch down.

Making the Aero Bat

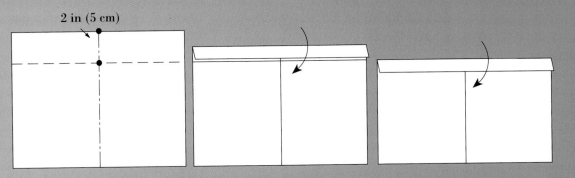

STEP 1 Lay the paper flat in a horizontal direction. Fold paper in half vertically, using the mountain fold. Unfold. Measure from upper edge and valley fold horizontally. Unfold. Then fold upper edge to meet horizontal crease. Refold original horizontal crease.

2 in (5 cm)

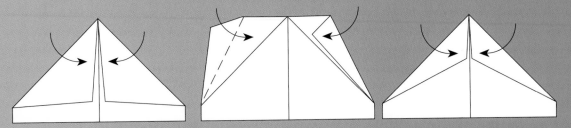

STEP 2 Valley fold upper corners to the vertical center crease. Unfold. Valley fold the upper corners to the diagonal creases. Then refold original diagonal creases.

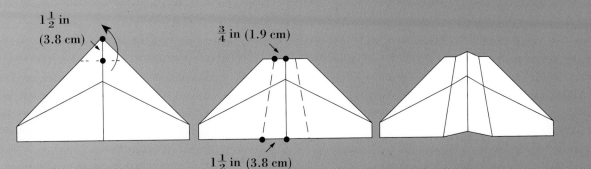

$1\frac{1}{2}$ in (3.8 cm)

$\frac{3}{4}$ in (1.9 cm)

$1\frac{1}{2}$ in (3.8 cm)

STEP 3 Measure from tip and mountain fold horizontally. On each side, measure and valley fold, as shown.

VIEW FROM BACK

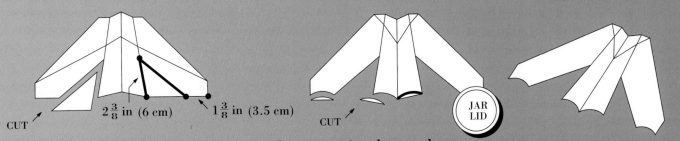

CUT

$2\frac{3}{8}$ in (6 cm) $1\frac{3}{8}$ in (3.5 cm)

CUT

JAR LID

STEP 4 On each side, measure and cut out triangles, as shown. Flip the airplane over. Then, using a small jar lid, trace scalloped edges and cut out, as shown. Adjust folds so that viewed from the back the plane forms an inverted W.

Sky Bird

HISTORICAL INFORMATION

The first aircraft had no engines. They were gliders. Early airplane builders used high hills as launching points to test their constructions. The builders soon realized that in order for airplanes to fly successfully, having wings was not enough. Airplanes also needed horizontal and vertical surfaces for stability. Otto Lilienthal made many successful glider flights in the 1890s. This paper airplane is modeled on early glider aircraft.

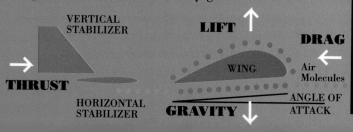

Technical Information

Drag This is the force of resistance that air gives when objects move through it. Because of drag it is hard work to pedal your bike very fast. Drag also acts on an airplane in flight. It is responsible for slowing down a paper airplane.

Thrust This is the forward momentum of an airplane. After you launch a paper airplane the force of lift prevents gravity from pulling the plane straight down, but gravity is still at work. In a glider, gravity provides thrust. In flight the nose should point down slightly. In gliding flight, gravity will pull the plane along an invisible mass of air in a gentle downward movement, just as gravity pulls a sled down a hill. If the nose is pointed down too much the plane will dive and crash into the ground.

The four forces – lift, gravity, thrust, and drag – are always present acting together on an airplane in flight.

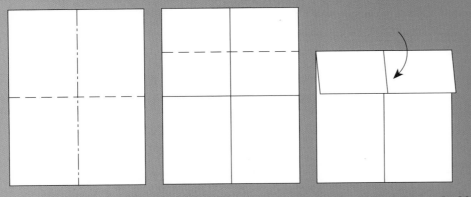

STEP 1 Lay paper flat in a vertical direction. Fold paper in half vertically using a mountain fold. Unfold. Valley fold the paper in half horizontally. Unfold. Then valley fold the top to meet the horizontal crease.

STEP 2 Valley fold the top again to meet the horizontal crease. Then valley fold top again, to meet the horizontal crease. Finally, applying glue to entire length, refold the original horizontal crease.

GLUE   GLUE

STEP 3 Flip over. Measure from top and draw line, as shown. On each side, measure and cut out along heavy lines to make wings and tail, as shown.

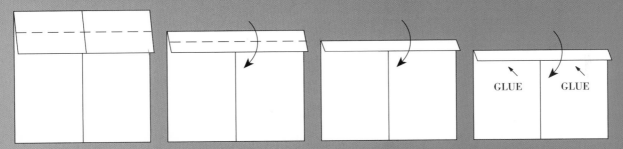

2 in
(5 cm)

$3\frac{1}{2}$ in
(8.9 cm)
CUT

$2\frac{3}{4}$ in
(7 cm)

CUT

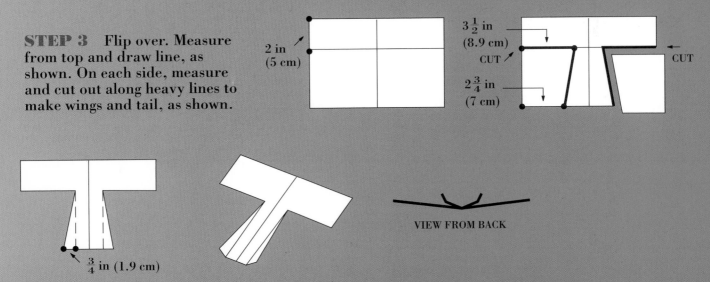

$\frac{3}{4}$ in (1.9 cm)

VIEW FROM BACK

STEP 4 On each side of tail, measure and valley fold. Adjust dihedral (upward slanting of wings and tail), as shown.

STEP 5 Cut the two pieces left over from step 3 into rectangles, as shown.

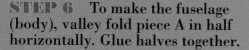

STEP 6 To make the fuselage (body), valley fold piece A in half horizontally. Glue halves together.

STEP 7 Valley fold this piece in half vertically. Then fold each vertical edge back to meet center crease. Glue center section. This is the fuselage.

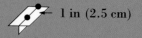

STEP 8 To make nose ballast, valley fold piece B in half horizontally. Glue halves together. Valley fold in half vertically. Glue halves together. Then valley fold in half horizontally. Glue halves together. Finally, valley fold in half vertically.

STEP 9 Glue this piece to the bottom of the center section of the fuselage, aligning at one of the ends. This end becomes the front.

1 in (2.5 cm)

STEP 10 Measure from front of fuselage and mark the point, as shown.

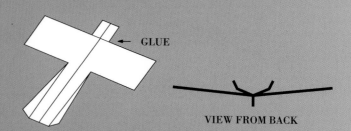

VIEW FROM BACK

STEP 11 Glue wings and tail to the fuselage with the leading edge (front of the wings) at the measured point. Make sure pieces are centered. Adjust dihedral (upward slanting of wings and tail) again.

Plain Plane

HISTORICAL INFORMATION

Achieving stability in flight was a major concern for early airplane designers, and remains so today. In the early days many different airplane shapes were tried. The most practical arrangement of parts had wings near the middle attached to a fuselage (body) with a tail at the back that had both horizontal and vertical surfaces. The fuselage also had room for the pilot. This arrangement has become the conventional and most often used aircraft design. Movable surfaces were added to the trailing (back) edges of wings and stabilizers: ailerons on the wing tips controlled roll (rotation along the length of an airplane), elevators on the horizontal tail controled pitch (nose up or down), and a rudder on the vertical tail controled yaw (nose left or right). This paper airplane is modeled on the conventional airplane.

Technical Information

If an airplane is to be stable in flight, it is important to get the center of gravity in the correct spot. (The planes in this book are designed with the correct center of gravity location, but if more ballast is needed, add it to the nose by using a small piece of paper, a dab of plasticine, some clear tape, or a small pin.) For best construction results use the 20 or 24 lb bond copier paper recommended, measure accurately, and make crisp folds. Use glue sparingly, but use enough to hold the parts together.

While an airplane is in flight the four forces (lift, gravity, thrust, and drag) must be in balance. Then the airplane is in trim for straight and level flight. Paper airplanes need frequent small adjustments to the control surfaces in order to fly well. You may need to make different trim adjustments for indoor flight than for outdoor flight in lively air. Always make small corrections. Remember, a small adjustment has a big effect.

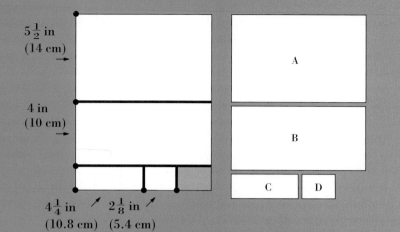

5 $\frac{1}{2}$ in
(14 cm)

4 in
(10 cm)

A

B

C   D

4 $\frac{1}{4}$ in   2 $\frac{1}{8}$ in
(10.8 cm)   (5.4 cm)

STEP 1   Measure and cut the various pieces from a sheet of bond paper, as shown.

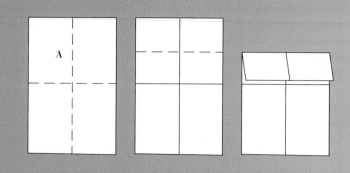

A

STEP 2   Lay piece A flat in a vertical direction. To make the fuselage, fold in half vertically using a valley fold. Unfold. Valley fold in half horizontally. Unfold. Then valley fold the top to meet the horizontal crease.

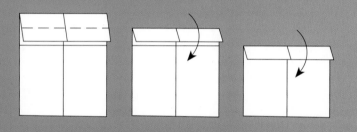

STEP 3   Valley fold the top again to meet the horizontal crease. Refold the original crease.

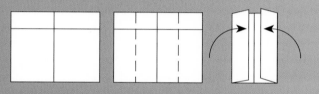

STEP 4   Valley fold each side so that outer edges meet center crease, as shown.

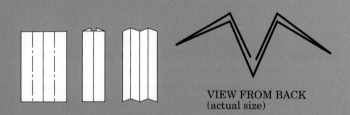

VIEW FROM BACK
(actual size)

STEP 5   Fold each side again using a mountain fold, so that outer edges meet center crease at back. Then adjust folds so the paper looks like an upside-down W, as shown.

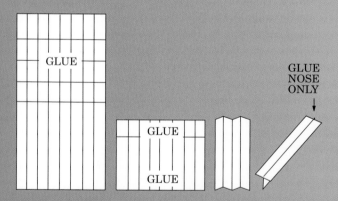

GLUE

GLUE

GLUE

GLUE
NOSE
ONLY

STEP 6   Unfold fuselage (piece A) completely. Refold applying glue to contacting surfaces, as shown. Make sure fuselage is straight.

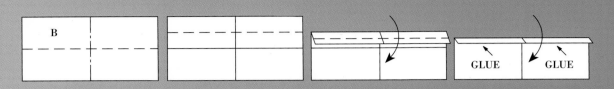

STEP 7 Use piece B to make the wings. Lay paper flat horizontally. Fold in half vertically, using a mountain fold. Unfold. Fold in half horizontally, using a valley fold. Unfold. Then valley fold so that top edge meets center crease. Fold again so that top edge meets center crease. Applying glue to entire length, refold original horizontal center crease. The folded over part is the bottom of the leading edge (front) of the wings.

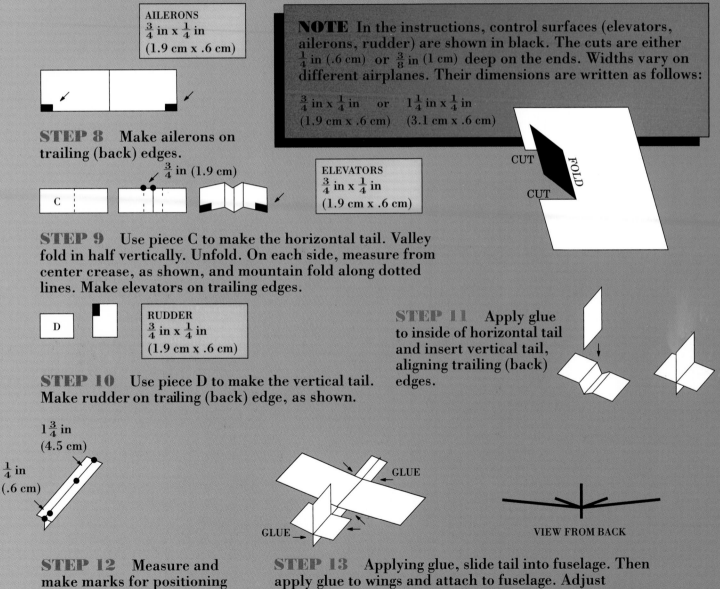

AILERONS
$\frac{3}{4}$ in x $\frac{1}{4}$ in
(1.9 cm x .6 cm)

NOTE In the instructions, control surfaces (elevators, ailerons, rudder) are shown in black. The cuts are either $\frac{1}{4}$ in (.6 cm) or $\frac{3}{8}$ in (1 cm) deep on the ends. Widths vary on different airplanes. Their dimensions are written as follows:

$\frac{3}{4}$ in x $\frac{1}{4}$ in or $1\frac{1}{4}$ in x $\frac{1}{4}$ in
(1.9 cm x .6 cm)   (3.1 cm x .6 cm)

STEP 8 Make ailerons on trailing (back) edges.

$\frac{3}{4}$ in (1.9 cm)

ELEVATORS
$\frac{3}{4}$ in x $\frac{1}{4}$ in
(1.9 cm x .6 cm)

STEP 9 Use piece C to make the horizontal tail. Valley fold in half vertically. Unfold. On each side, measure from center crease, as shown, and mountain fold along dotted lines. Make elevators on trailing edges.

RUDDER
$\frac{3}{4}$ in x $\frac{1}{4}$ in
(1.9 cm x .6 cm)

STEP 11 Apply glue to inside of horizontal tail and insert vertical tail, aligning trailing (back) edges.

STEP 10 Use piece D to make the vertical tail. Make rudder on trailing (back) edge, as shown.

$1\frac{3}{4}$ in
(4.5 cm)

$\frac{1}{4}$ in
(.6 cm)

GLUE

GLUE

VIEW FROM BACK

STEP 12 Measure and make marks for positioning tail and wings.

STEP 13 Applying glue, slide tail into fuselage. Then apply glue to wings and attach to fuselage. Adjust dihedral (upward slanting of wings and tail).

Biplane

HISTORICAL INFORMATION

One way to improve lift without making large wings was by having two sets of them, one above the other (biplanes). The box-like construction of these airplanes made it easy to cross-brace the lightweight wooden frames with wire for strength. In 1903 Orville and Wilbur Wright put an engine into a biplane and became the first to attain sustained powered flight. Biplanes were used for most of the air battles of World War I, which began in 1914. Fighter biplanes were highly maneuverable although difficult to handle. Some examples are the Spad 7, Sopwith Camel, and Fokker 7. Biplanes are now used where small, durable, and maneuverable airplanes are required. Crop spraying is a good example. This paper airplane is modeled on early biplanes.

Technical Information

Biplanes have stubby noses and short wings and tails, making them sensitive to pitch and roll because the distances from the center of gravity to the control surfaces are small. The planes require careful trimming.

If the airplane zooms nose down to the ground, bend the elevators up slightly to raise the nose in flight.

This may cause the nose of the plane to pitch up sharply. As a result the air no longer flows smoothly over the wing surfaces but separates into eddies and the wings stall. To solve this problem bend the elevators up less.

If the elevators are not bent at all and the nose still rises, don't bend the elevators down to correct the problem (a plane should never fly this way). Rather add a bit of extra ballast to the nose.

If the plane veers to left or right, bend the aileron up slightly on the wing that rises and down slightly on the wing that falls. Also bend the rudder on the vertical tail slightly, opposite to the direction of the turn.

Making the Biplane

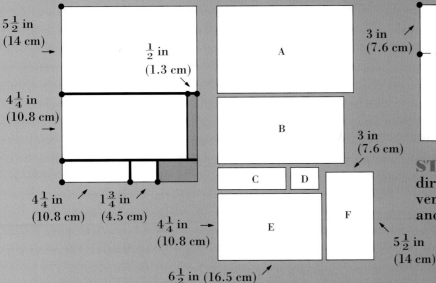

5 ½ in (14 cm)

½ in (1.3 cm)

4 ¼ in (10.8 cm)

A

B

C   D

E

F

4 ¼ in (10.8 cm)   1 ¾ in (4.5 cm)

4 ¼ in (10.8 cm)

6 ½ in (16.5 cm)

3 in (7.6 cm)

3 in (7.6 cm)

5 ½ in (14 cm)

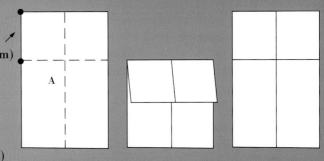

STEP 2   Lay piece A flat in a vertical direction. To make the fuselage, fold in half vertically using a valley fold. Unfold. Measure and valley fold horizontally, as shown. Unfold.

STEP 1   Measure and cut the various pieces from a sheet of bond paper, as shown. Two additional pieces E and F are needed, as shown.

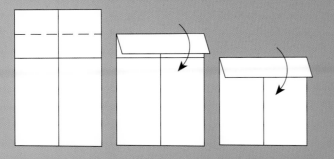

STEP 3   Valley fold the top to meet the horizontal crease. Then refold the original horizontal crease.

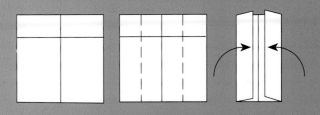

STEP 4   Valley fold each side so that outer edges meet center crease, as shown.

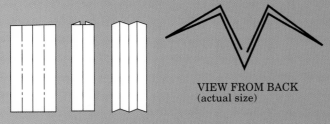

VIEW FROM BACK
(actual size)

STEP 5   Fold each side again using a mountain fold, so that outer edges meet center crease at back. Then adjust folds so that paper looks like an upside-down W, as shown.

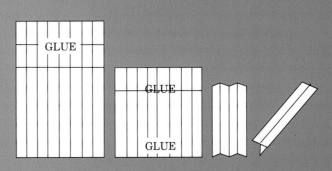

GLUE

GLUE

GLUE

STEP 6   Unfold fuselage completely. Refold applying glue to all contacting surfaces, as shown. Make sure fuselage is straight. Do not glue nose yet.

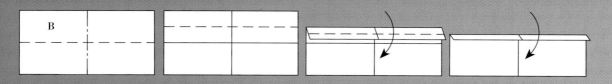

STEP 7   Lay piece B in a horizontal position to make the lower wings. Fold in half vertically, using a mountain fold. Unfold. Fold in half horizontally, using a valley fold. Unfold. Then valley fold so that top edge meets center crease. Fold again so that top edge meets center crease. Refold original horizontal center crease.

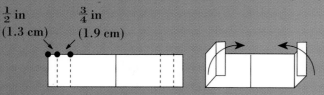

$1\frac{5}{8}$ in (4.1 cm)

STEP 8   Unfold completely. On each side, measure and cut diagonally, as shown. Refold. Apply glue before refolding original horizontal center crease only. The folded over part is the bottom of the leading edge (front) of the wings.

$\frac{1}{2}$ in (1.3 cm) $\frac{3}{4}$ in (1.9 cm)

STEP 9   On each side, measure and valley fold, as shown.

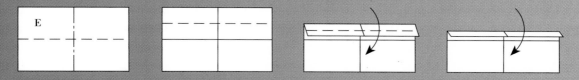

STEP 10   Lay piece E horizontally to make the upper wings. Fold in half vertically, using a mountain fold. Unfold. Fold in half horizontally, using a valley fold. Unfold. Then valley fold so that top edge meets center crease. Fold again so that top edge meets center crease. Refold original horizontal center crease.

2 in (5 cm)

STEP 11   Unfold completely. On each side, measure and cut diagonally, as shown. Refold. Apply glue before refolding original horizontal center crease only. The folded over part is the bottom of the leading edge (front) of the wings.

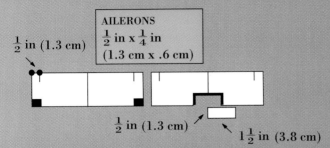

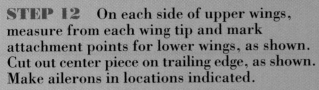

AILERONS
$\frac{1}{2}$ in x $\frac{1}{4}$ in
(1.3 cm x .6 cm)

$\frac{1}{2}$ in (1.3 cm)

$\frac{1}{2}$ in (1.3 cm)

$1\frac{1}{2}$ in (3.8 cm)

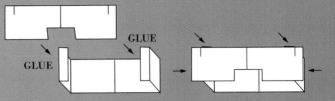

GLUE

GLUE

STEP 12 On each side of upper wings, measure from each wing tip and mark attachment points for lower wings, as shown. Cut out center piece on trailing edge, as shown. Make ailerons in locations indicated.

STEP 13 Applying glue, fasten upper and lower wings together, as shown. Make sure both leading edges face the same direction.

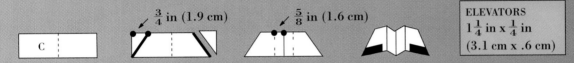

$\frac{3}{4}$ in (1.9 cm)

$\frac{5}{8}$ in (1.6 cm)

ELEVATORS
$1\frac{1}{4}$ in x $\frac{1}{4}$ in
(3.1 cm x .6 cm)

STEP 14 Use piece C to make the horizontal tail. Valley fold in half vertically. Unfold. On each side, measure from outer edges, as shown, and cut along heavy lines. Then, on each side, measure from center crease and mountain fold, as shown. Make elevators.

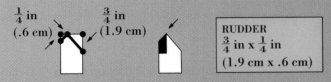

$\frac{1}{4}$ in (.6 cm)

$\frac{3}{4}$ in (1.9 cm)

RUDDER
$\frac{3}{4}$ in x $\frac{1}{4}$ in
(1.9 cm x .6 cm)

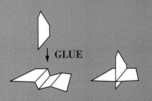

GLUE

STEP 15 Measure and cut leading edge along heavy lines, as shown. On trailing edge, make rudder.

STEP 16 Apply glue to inside of horizontal tail and insert vertical tail, aligning trailing (back) edges.

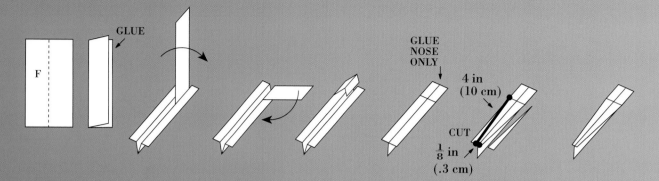

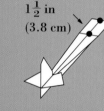

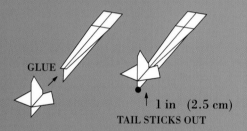

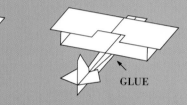

STEP 17 Use piece F to make the nose cowl (ballast). Valley fold piece in half vertically. Glue halves together. Applying glue to one side, insert F into nose and wrap entirely around fuselage, as shown. Then glue fuselage together at nose only.

STEP 18 On each side, measure and cut fuselage back along heavy lines, as shown.

GLUE

1 in   (2.5 cm)

TAIL STICKS OUT

$1\frac{1}{2}$ in (3.8 cm)

GLUE

STEP 19 Applying glue, slide the tail into the back of the fuselelage.

STEP 20 Measure from front of fuselage and mark front of wing position. Glue wings in place, as shown.

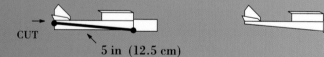

CUT

5 in (12.5 cm)

VIEW FROM BACK

STEP 21 Measure and cut back of fuselage, as shown. Adjust dihedral (upward slanting of wings and tail) to finish airplane.

Aero Stunt

HISTORICAL INFORMATION

Ever since the earliest days of flight, flying events attracted great crowds of spectators. After World War I, many pilots performed aerial maneuvers learned in combat as stunts for entertainment. Sometimes people walked on the wings, or even jumped from one plane to another, while the airplanes were in flight. Such events (called barnstorming) thrilled spectators, and even today, air shows where aerobatics are performed, draw huge crowds. As planes improved, air racing became popular. Speeds exceeded 200 mph. This paper airplane is designed specifically to do stunts. It will not fly straight and level.

Technical Information

Loops When an airplane flies a loop it must maintain its speed throughout the entire maneuver. Making a round loop depends on centrifugal force. This force pushes the plane outwards, much like swinging a ball on a string. Only there is no string to hold it. Instead, the plane's wings create a centripedal force that keeps it from flying off and distorting the loop.

Rolls When the ailerons are used, one bends upwards and the other one bends down. This causes the airplane to bank in the direction of the upward bent aileron. A powered airplane can roll completely, over and over, flying along in corkscrew fashion.

Hammerheads In this maneuver the airplane is flown straight up, but before it stalls the plane is turned so that it points straight down, swooping smoothly out of the dive.

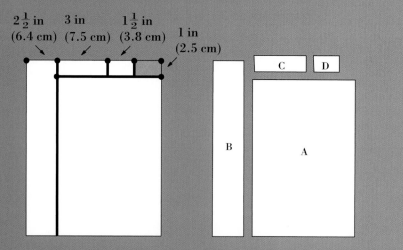

2½ in (6.4 cm) 3 in (7.5 cm) 1½ in (3.8 cm) 1 in (2.5 cm)

C D

B A

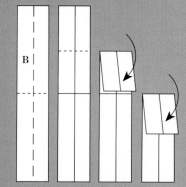

B

STEP 1 Measure and cut four pieces from a sheet of bond paper, as shown.

STEP 2 Lay piece B vertically to make the fuselage. Valley fold in half vertically. Unfold. Valley fold in half horizontally. Unfold. Valley fold so that upper edge meets the horizontal crease. Then refold the original horizontal crease.

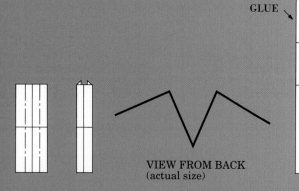

VIEW FROM BACK
(actual size)

GLUE

GLUE

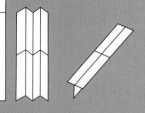

STEP 3 Fold each side using a mountain fold so that outer edges meet center crease at back. Then adjust folds so that paper looks like an upside-down W, as shown.

STEP 4 Unfold fuselage completely. Refold applying glue to all contacting surfaces, as shown. Make sure fuselage is straight.

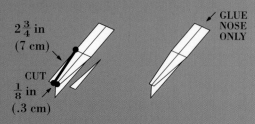

2¾ in (7 cm)

CUT

⅛ in (.3 cm)

GLUE NOSE ONLY

STEP 5 On each side, measure and cut fuselage back along heavy lines, as shown. Then glue nose only.

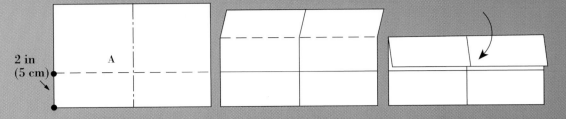

2 in
(5 cm)

A

STEP 6   Lay piece A horizontally to make the wings. Fold in half vertically, using a mountain fold. Unfold. Measure from the bottom and fold horizontally, using a valley fold. Unfold. Then valley fold so that top edge meets horizontal crease.

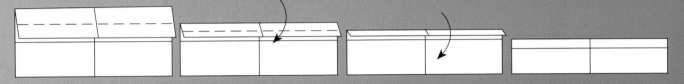

STEP 7   Valley fold so that top edge meets horizontal crease. Again valley fold so that top edge meets horizontal crease. Then refold original horizontal crease.

NOTE: Control surfaces for this plane are different from all the others.

GLUE

$\frac{1}{2}$ in
(1.3 cm)

$\frac{1}{2}$ in
(1.3 cm)

$\frac{1}{2}$ in (1.3 cm)

$\frac{1}{2}$ in
(1.3 cm)

C

STEP 8   Unfold the last fold only and apply glue to entire length. Refold. Make ailerons by folding diagonally, as shown.

STEP 9   Use piece C to make the horizontal tail. Valley fold in half vertically. Unfold. On each side, measure from center crease and mountain fold, as shown. Make elevators by folding diagonally, as shown.

$\frac{1}{2}$ in (1.3 cm)

$\frac{1}{2}$ in
(1.3 cm)

D

GLUE

STEP 10   Use piece D for the vertical tail. Measure and cut diagonally along heavy line, as shown. Then apply glue to inside of horizontal tail and insert vertical tail, aligning trailing (back) edges.

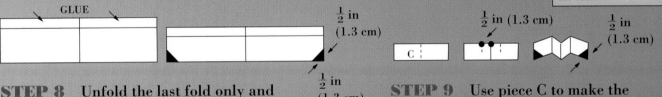

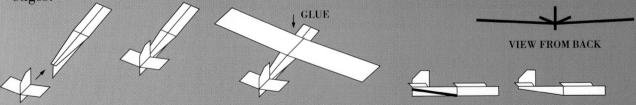

GLUE

VIEW FROM BACK

STEP 11   Applying glue, slide the tail into the back of fuselage, aligning trailing edges.

STEP 12   Applying glue, attach wings so that trailing edges align with seam on the fuselage.

STEP 13   Cut fuselage diagonally from the seam to the back, as shown by heavy line. Adjust dihedral (upward slanting of wings and tail), as shown.

Gee Bee Racer

HISTORICAL INFORMATION

From the very beginning of powered flight, it became apparent that airplanes and speed belonged together. Air races were established so that builders could compete with one another. Three popular races were the Thompson Race, the Bendix Race, and the Shell Speed Dash. In 1932 the Granville brothers built the Gee Bee model R racer to compete in all three races. Two R models were built. That year they won the Thompson and set a new Speed Dash record of almost 300 mph. It takes great skill to fly at high speed near the ground in a tempermental airplane such as a racer. Both planes eventually crashed, and two pilots lost their lives. Today another Gee Bee, just like the originals, has been built. It is a popular attraction at many air shows.

Technical Information

The Gee Bee model R is mostly a flying engine. Its big radial engine produces over 500 horsepower. Drag is the enemy of the racer. To go fast, even with a powerful engine, drag must be kept at a minimum. When this plane was being designed, different shapes were tested in a wind tunnel to find a shape that had the least amount of drag. A fat and stubby "teardrop" shape was found to be ideal. But such a stubby shape makes for a tempermental plane to fly. All airplanes that are stubby with short wings and tails are sensitive to pitch and roll because the distances from the center of gravity to the control surfaces are short. This paper model, however, is a remarkably good flyer.

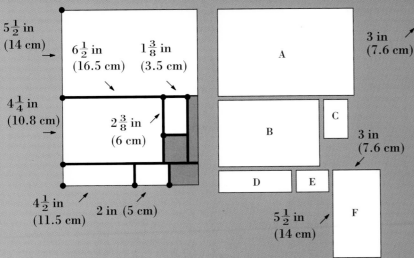

5 ½ in
(14 cm)

6 ½ in
(16.5 cm)

1 ⅜ in
(3.5 cm)

4 ¼ in
(10.8 cm)

2 ⅜ in
(6 cm)

4 ½ in
(11.5 cm)

2 in (5 cm)

A

B

C

D   E

3 in
(7.6 cm)

F

5 ½ in
(14 cm)

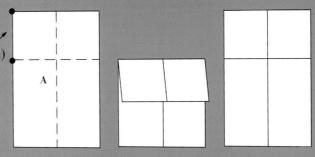

3 in
(7.6 cm)

A

3 in
(7.6 cm)

STEP 2   Lay piece A flat in a vertical direction. Fold in half vertically using a valley fold, to make the fuselage. Unfold. Measure and valley fold horizontally, as shown. Unfold.

STEP 1   Measure and cut the various pieces from a sheet of bond paper, as shown. One additional piece F is needed, as shown.

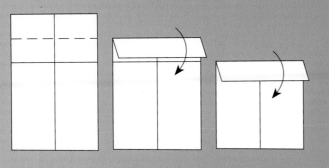

STEP 3   Valley fold the top to meet the horizontal crease. Then refold the original horizontal crease.

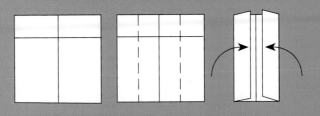

STEP 4   Valley fold each side so that outer edges meet center crease, as shown.

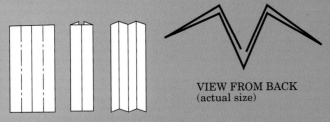

VIEW FROM BACK
(actual size)

STEP 5   Fold each side again using a mountain fold, so that outer edges meet center crease at back. Then adjust folds so that paper looks like an upside-down W, as shown.

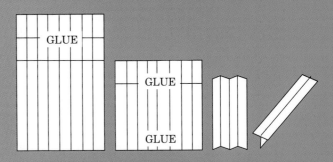

GLUE

GLUE

GLUE

STEP 6   Unfold fuselage completely. Refold applying glue to all contacting surfaces, as shown. Make sure fuselage is straight. Do not glue nose yet.

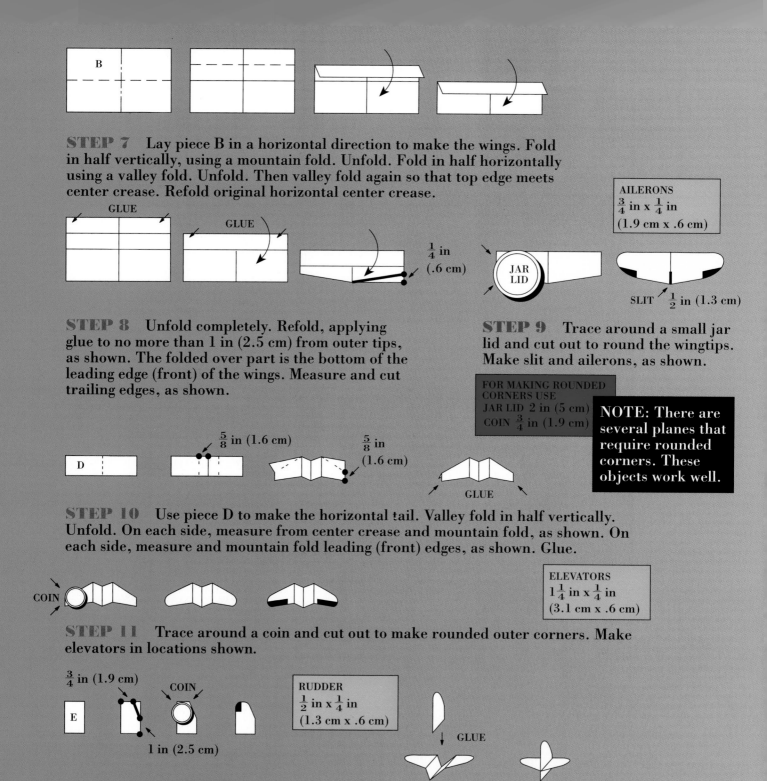

STEP 7 Lay piece B in a horizontal direction to make the wings. Fold in half vertically, using a mountain fold. Unfold. Fold in half horizontally using a valley fold. Unfold. Then valley fold again so that top edge meets center crease. Refold original horizontal center crease.

GLUE

GLUE

$\frac{1}{4}$ in (.6 cm)

AILERONS
$\frac{3}{4}$ in x $\frac{1}{4}$ in
(1.9 cm x .6 cm)

JAR LID

SLIT $\frac{1}{2}$ in (1.3 cm)

STEP 8 Unfold completely. Refold, applying glue to no more than 1 in (2.5 cm) from outer tips, as shown. The folded over part is the bottom of the leading edge (front) of the wings. Measure and cut trailing edges, as shown.

STEP 9 Trace around a small jar lid and cut out to round the wingtips. Make slit and ailerons, as shown.

FOR MAKING ROUNDED CORNERS USE
JAR LID 2 in (5 cm)
COIN $\frac{3}{4}$ in (1.9 cm)

NOTE: There are several planes that require rounded corners. These objects work well.

$\frac{5}{8}$ in (1.6 cm)

$\frac{5}{8}$ in (1.6 cm)

GLUE

STEP 10 Use piece D to make the horizontal tail. Valley fold in half vertically. Unfold. On each side, measure from center crease and mountain fold, as shown. On each side, measure and mountain fold leading (front) edges, as shown. Glue.

COIN

ELEVATORS
$1\frac{1}{4}$ in x $\frac{1}{4}$ in
(3.1 cm x .6 cm)

STEP 11 Trace around a coin and cut out to make rounded outer corners. Make elevators in locations shown.

$\frac{3}{4}$ in (1.9 cm)

COIN

1 in (2.5 cm)

RUDDER
$\frac{1}{2}$ in x $\frac{1}{4}$ in
(1.3 cm x .6 cm)

GLUE

STEP 12 Use piece E to make the vertical tail. Measure and cut leading (front) edge as shown by heavy line. Trace around a coin and cut out to round corners. On trailing edge, make rudder.

STEP 13 Apply glue to inside of horizontal tail and insert vertical tail, aligning trailing (back) edges.

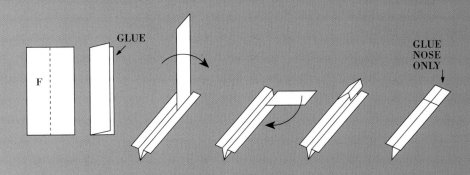

STEP 14 Use piece F to make the nose cowl (ballast). Valley fold piece in half vertically. Glue halves together. Applying glue to one side, insert F into nose and wrap entirely around fuselage, as shown. Then glue fuselage together at nose only.

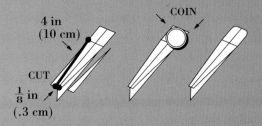

STEP 15 On each side, measure and cut fuselage back along heavy lines, as shown. Trace around a coin and cut out to round the nose.

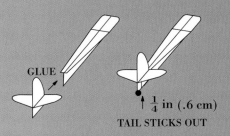

STEP 16 Applying glue, slide the tail into the back of the fuselage.

STEP 17 Measure from front of fuselage and mark front of wing position. Glue wings in place, as shown.

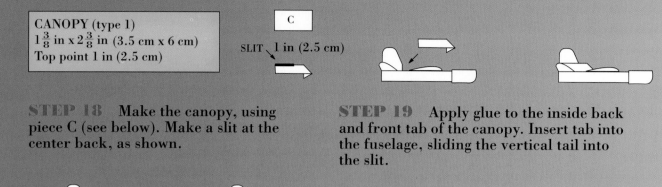

CANOPY (type 1)
$1\frac{3}{8}$ in x $2\frac{3}{8}$ in (3.5 cm x 6 cm)
Top point 1 in (2.5 cm)

C

SLIT 1 in (2.5 cm)

STEP 18 Make the canopy, using piece C (see below). Make a slit at the center back, as shown.

STEP 19 Apply glue to the inside back and front tab of the canopy. Insert tab into the fuselage, sliding the vertical tail into the slit.

CUT

5 in (12.5 cm)

VIEW FROM BACK

STEP 20 Measure and cut back of fuselage, as shown. Adjust dihedral (upward slanting of wings and tail) to finish airplane.

NOTE This is the first airplane design in this book to have a canopy. The canopy adds realism as well as ballast. There are two main types, as shown below. Dimensions are given with each airplane design.

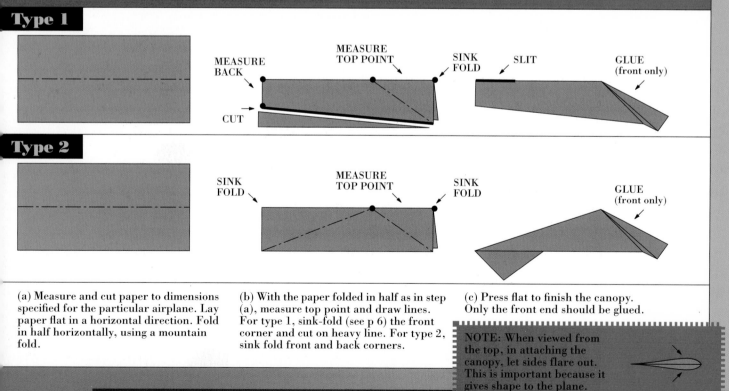

Type 1

MEASURE
BACK

MEASURE
TOP POINT

SINK
FOLD

SLIT

GLUE
(front only)

CUT

Type 2

SINK
FOLD

MEASURE
TOP POINT

SINK
FOLD

GLUE
(front only)

(a) Measure and cut paper to dimensions specified for the particular airplane. Lay paper flat in a horizontal direction. Fold in half horizontally, using a mountain fold.

(b) With the paper folded in half as in step (a), measure top point and draw lines. For type 1, sink-fold (see p 6) the front corner and cut on heavy line. For type 2, sink fold front and back corners.

(c) Press flat to finish the canopy. Only the front end should be glued.

NOTE: When viewed from the top, in attaching the canopy, let sides flare out. This is important because it gives shape to the plane.

28

P47 Thunderbolt

HISTORICAL INFORMATION

With the outbreak of another world war in 1939, there was again a demand for maneuverable fighter planes. Streamlined airframes capable of great speed were designed. More powerful engines were made, pushing speeds past 400 mph. Some popular examples of fighters are the Republic P47, North American P51, Supermarine Spitfire, Messerschmitt ME109, and the Mitsubishi "Zero". After the war ended in 1945 some of these warplanes became sport planes, and these inspired the building of aircraft using aerodynamic and technical information gained from fighter design. This paper airplane is modeled on the fighters of World War II and present-day sport planes.

Technical Information

Speed and Drag: From the very beginning of powered flight it was realized that speed and flight belonged together. The unobstructed freedom that flying offered, combined with speed, made it easy and fast to get from place to place. The biplanes of World War I, with engines about as powerful as those found in a small car, could exceed 100 mph. The fighters of World War II, with much more powerful engines, could exceed 400 mph. With such an increase in speed, drag also increased and airplane builders had to find ways to reduce it as much as possible. One way was by rounding corners and removing things that stuck out into the airflow (streamlining) and hiding them underneath a smooth skin.

In slow flight (as in landing) airplanes that can fly fast need a method of increasing the lift of their high-speed wings. They have secondary control surfaces, called flaps, that bend down on the trailing edges of the wings near the fuselage. Flaps are used not only when landing but also for takeoff or whenever extra lift is needed.

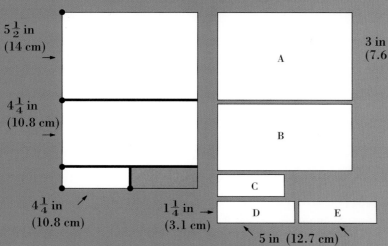

5 1/2 in (14 cm)

4 1/4 in (10.8 cm)

4 1/4 in (10.8 cm)

1 1/4 in (3.1 cm)

5 in (12.7 cm)

A

B

C

D

E

STEP 1 Measure and cut the various pieces from a sheet of bond paper, as shown. Two additional pieces D and E are needed, as shown.

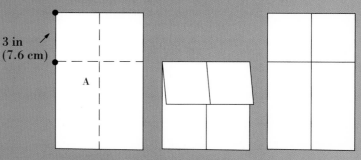

3 in (7.6 cm)

A

STEP 2 Lay piece A flat in a vertical direction to make the fuselage. Fold in half vertically using a valley fold. Unfold. Measure and valley fold horizontally, as shown. Unfold.

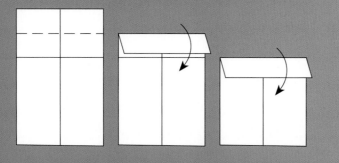

STEP 3 Valley fold the top to meet the horizontal crease. Then refold the original horizontal crease.

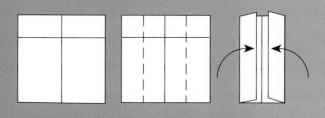

STEP 4 Valley fold each side so that outer edges meet center crease, as shown.

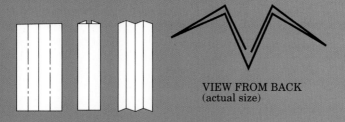

VIEW FROM BACK
(actual size)

STEP 5 Fold each side again using a mountain fold, so that outer edges meet center crease at back. Then adjust folds so that paper looks like an upside-down W, as shown.

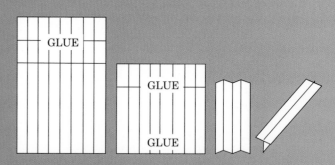

GLUE

GLUE

GLUE

STEP 6 Unfold fuselage completely. Refold applying glue to all contacting surfaces, as shown. Make sure fuselage is straight. Do not glue nose yet.

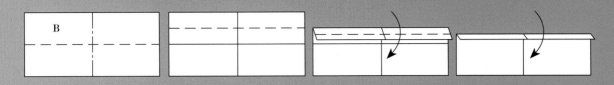

STEP 7   Lay piece B horizontally to make the wings. Fold in half vertically, using a mountain fold. Unfold. Fold in half horizontally, using a valley fold. Unfold. Then valley fold so that top edge meets center crease. Fold again so that top edge meets center crease. Refold original horizontal center crease.

$1\frac{5}{8}$ in
(4.1 cm)

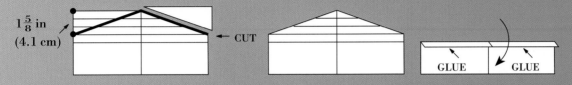

STEP 8   Unfold completely. On each side, measure and cut diagonally, as shown. Refold. Apply glue before refolding original horizontal center crease only. The folded over part is the bottom of the leading edge (front) of the wings.

$1\frac{5}{8}$ in
(4.1 cm)

STEP 9   Measure and cut trailing edge (back) of wings, as shown. Trace around a coin to make rounded corners at the leading edges and a small jar lid for the trailing edge, and cut out (see p 26). Make ailerons, as shown.

$1\frac{1}{4}$ in (3.1 cm)

AILERONS
1 in x $\frac{1}{4}$ in
(2.5 cm x .6 cm)

NOTE: In the instructions, secondary control surfaces (flaps) are shown in red.

FLAPS
$1\frac{1}{4}$ in x $\frac{1}{4}$ in
(3.1 cm x .6 cm)

STEP 10   On trailing edges, make ailerons. Then make secondary control surfaces (flaps), in locations shown.

$\frac{5}{8}$ in (1.6 cm)

$\frac{3}{4}$ in (1.9 cm)

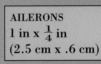 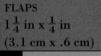

GLUE

STEP 11   Use piece D to make the horizontal tail. Valley fold in half vertically. Unfold. On each side, measure from center crease, as shown, and mountain fold. On each side, measure and mountain fold leading (front) edges, as shown. Glue.

ELEVATORS
$1\frac{1}{2}$ in x $\frac{1}{4}$ in
(3.8 cm x .6 cm)

STEP 12   Trace around a coin and cut out to make all the corners rounded (see p 26). Make elevators, as shown.

E

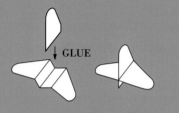

← GLUE

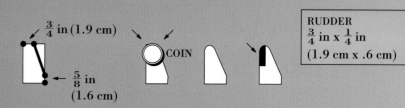

$\frac{3}{4}$ in (1.9 cm)

$\frac{5}{8}$ in (1.6 cm)

COIN

RUDDER
$\frac{3}{4}$ in x $\frac{1}{4}$ in
(1.9 cm x .6 cm)

STEP 13 Use piece E to make the vertical tail. Mountain fold in half horizontally, glue halves together.

STEP 14 Measure and cut leading edge along heavy line, as shown. Trace around a coin and cut out to round corners (see p 26). On trailing (back) edge, make rudder.

GLUE

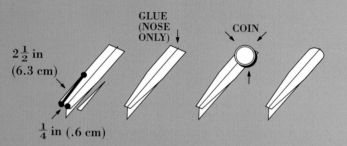

GLUE (NOSE ONLY)

COIN

$2\frac{1}{2}$ in (6.3 cm)

$\frac{1}{4}$ in (.6 cm)

STEP 15 Apply glue to inside of horizontal tail and insert vertical tail, aligning trailing (back) edges.

STEP 16 On each side, measure and cut fuselage back, as shown. Then glue nose only. To round corners, trace around a coin and cut out all corners of the nose (see p 26).

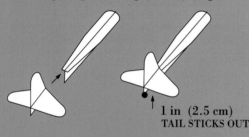

1 in (2.5 cm)
TAIL STICKS OUT

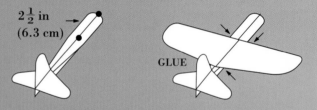

$2\frac{1}{2}$ in (6.3 cm)

GLUE

STEP 17 Applying glue, slide the tail into back of fuselage.

STEP 18 Measure from front of fuselage and glue wings in place, as shown.

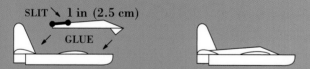

SLIT   1 in (2.5 cm)

GLUE

CANOPY (type 1)
$1\frac{1}{4}$ in x $4\frac{1}{4}$ in (3.1 cm x 10.8 cm)
Top point 1 in (2.5 cm)
Back $\frac{3}{8}$ in (1 cm)

STEP 19 Make a type 1 canopy, using piece C (See p 28). Cut slit in back of canopy. Apply glue to inside back of canopy and the front tab. Slip back over vertical tail and front tab into fuselage, as shown.

CUT

4 in (10 cm)

VIEW FROM BACK

STEP 20 Measure and cut back of fuselage along heavy line, as shown. Adjust dihedral (upward slanting of wings and tail), as shown.

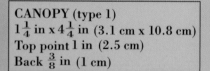

DH108 Swallow

HISTORICAL INFORMATION

Beyond a certain speed conventional airplanes become less controllable and propellers lose their efficiency. When aircraft approach the speed of sound (about 760 mph) their control becomes unpredictable due to air resistance. For high speed flight a new shape of airplane was needed. For propulsion, designers turned to rockets and jets, which don't need propellers. In the quest for greater speed, Messerschmitt experimented with a rocket propelled airplane during the war, the ME163. After the war, deHavilland used the information gained to build the similar, but jet engined, experimental DH108 Swallow. It had wings that swept back and no horizontal stabilizers. In 1946 it flew over 600 mph. This paper airplane is modeled on the deHavilland Swallow.

Technical Information

Sweepback: Every increase in speed increases drag. Below a speed of about 250 mph air molecules easily move around a well streamlined airplane's surfaces. As speed is increased, however, the molecules cannot move out of the way quickly enough and their resistance piles them up into a pressure ridge ahead of the wings, something like a snowplow pushing snow. This build-up of pressure (drag) makes it difficult to fly the airplane, and at the speed of sound it can become dangerous. Sweeping the wings back away from the fuselage and making them broader delayed the pressure build-up until a greater speed was reached. This resulted in wings that maintain their efficiency, safely allowing planes to fly faster.

The experimental Swallow was built to test high speed flight. But even with swept-back wings, when this plane reached the speed of sound, the pressure build-up was great enough to break the airplane, and it crashed.

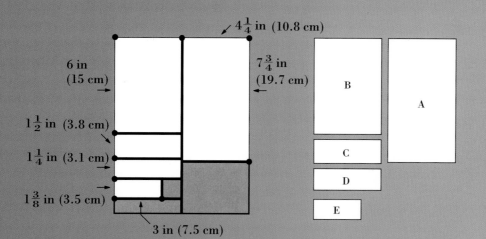

6 in (15 cm)

4¼ in (10.8 cm)

7¾ in (19.7 cm)

1½ in (3.8 cm)

1¼ in (3.1 cm)

1⅜ in (3.5 cm)

3 in (7.5 cm)

B

A

C

D

E

STEP 1 Measure and cut the various pieces, as shown.

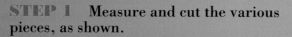

A

STEP 2 Lay piece A flat in a vertical direction. To make the fuselage, fold in half vertically using a valley fold. Unfold.

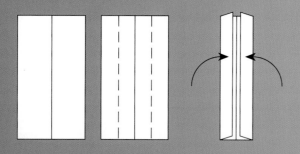

STEP 3 Valley fold each outer edge to meet center crease, as shown.

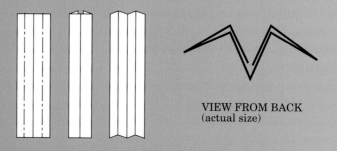

VIEW FROM BACK (actual size)

STEP 4 Fold each side again using a mountain fold, so that outer edges meet center crease at back. Then adjust folds so that paper looks like an upside-down W, as shown.

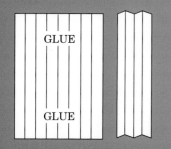

GLUE

GLUE

STEP 5 Unfold fuselage completely. Refold applying glue to all contacting surfaces, as shown. Make sure fuselage is straight.

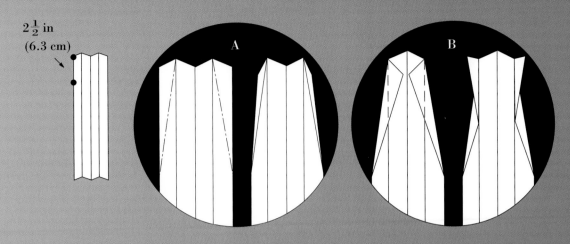

$2\frac{1}{2}$ in (6.3 cm)

A

B

STEP 6 On each side, measure from top (front of fuselage) and mountain fold along broken lines, as shown in enlarged view A. Then flip over fuselage. On each side, valley fold triangle along broken lines, matching fold line to existing crease, as shown in enlarged view B.

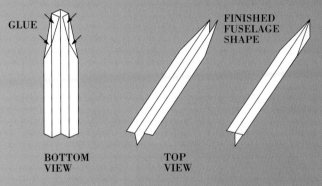

GLUE

FINISHED
FUSELAGE
SHAPE

BOTTOM
VIEW

TOP
VIEW

STEP 7 Glue triangles. Hold in place until glue sets. It is important that the fuselage stays straight. Do not glue nose yet.

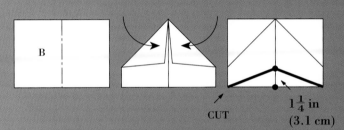

B

CUT

$1\frac{1}{4}$ in (3.1 cm)

STEP 8 Use piece B to make the wings. Lay paper flat in a horizontal direction. Mountain fold in half vertically. Unfold. Then fold each side diagonally so that upper edges meet center crease. Unfold. Measure and cut trailing (back) edge, as shown by heavy line.

AILERONS	ELEVATORS
$\frac{1}{2}$ in x $\frac{1}{4}$ in	$\frac{3}{4}$ in x $\frac{1}{4}$ in
(1.3 cm x .6 cm)	(1.9 cm x .6 cm)

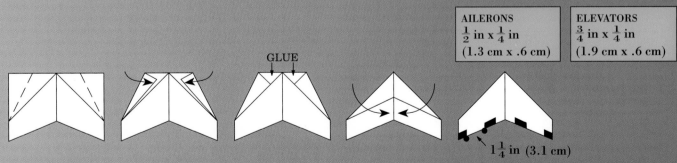

GLUE

$1\frac{1}{4}$ in (3.1 cm)

STEP 9 On each side, valley fold diagonally so that outer edge meets previously made diagonal crease. Then apply glue to upper tip only and refold along original diagonal creases.

STEP 10 Flip wings over. On each side, make ailerons and elevators in locations shown.

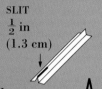

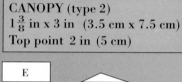

GLUE

$\frac{3}{4}$ in (1.9 cm)

$\frac{1}{2}$ in (1.3 cm)

STEP 11 Use piece C to make the vertical tail. Lay paper flat in a vertical direction. Mountain fold in half horizontally. Glue halves together.

STEP 12 Measure and cut, as shown. Make rudder in locations shown.

SLIT
$\frac{1}{2}$ in
(1.3 cm)

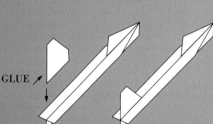

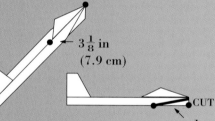

BACK VIEW
(actual size)

STEP 13 Use piece D to make the fuselage top. Mountain fold in half horizontally. Unfold. Then valley fold so that the outer edges meet center crease. Unfold. At one end, cut slit along center crease, as indicated by heavy line. Shape folds as shown.

STEP 14 Use piece E to make the canopy. (See p 28).

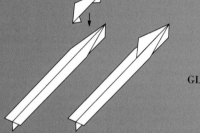

GLUE

$3\frac{1}{8}$ in
(7.9 cm)

CUT

$2\frac{1}{2}$ in
(6.3 cm)

STEP 15 Apply glue to inside of fuselage at the nose end and insert tabs on the bottom of canopy, aligning at the front. Hold until glue sets.

STEP 16 Apply glue to bottom part of vertical tail and insert into back of fuselage, aligning at the back edge.

STEP 17 Measure from front of fuselage and mark where to position wings. Measure and cut nose, as shown by heavy line.

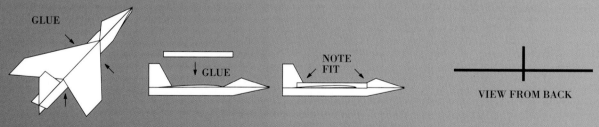

GLUE

GLUE

NOTE
FIT

VIEW FROM BACK

STEP 18 Glue wings to fuselage. Then glue top of fuselage in place so that slit fits around tail and front fits snuggly over back of canopy.

X1 Experimental

HISTORICAL INFORMATION

Some people believed that the speed of sound was a barrier that would never be crossed. But designers did not abandon their quest. They shaped an airplane like a 50 caliber bullet, which was known to travel faster than the speed of sound. This experimental plane was the stubby-winged Bell X1. It was called "Glamorous Glennis" after the pilot's wife. While this plane did not have swept-back wings, it successfully "broke the sound barrier" for the first time in 1947. Thus began the building of a long series of X planes used for experiments in ultra high speed and high altitude flight. The X15, for example, flew 8 times the speed of sound to the edge of space at an altitude of 70 miles (112 km) in 1956. This paper airplane is modeled on the Bell X1.

Technical Information

Sound Barrier: What we hear as different sounds are actually differences in air pressure that strike our eardrums. These waves of air (called sound waves) travel at about 760 mph. An airplane traveling at that speed creates a tremendous pressure ridge because so many air molecules are piled up ahead of its leading edges. What makes it so dangerous is that as speed increases, the ridge of pressure moves farther back over the wings and begins to affect the control surfaces which are on the trailing edges. Airplanes that successfully fly faster than the speed of sound must be designed so that the pressure is deflected in such a way that it does not affect aircraft control. Thus, their noses are pointed and their wings are thin, and either tapered or swept back. The planes must also be built strong enough to withstand the pressure. When supersonic airplanes break the sound barrier they create a loud booming noise (like a clap of thunder), as heard from the ground.

The speed of sound is also called Mach 1, twice that speed Mach 2, three times Mach 3, and so on, in honor of the scientist Ernst Mach.

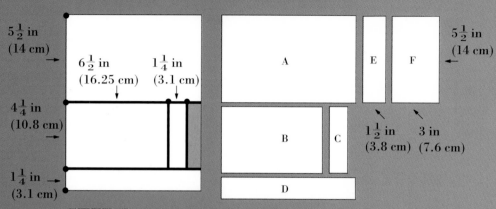

$5\frac{1}{2}$ in (14 cm)

$6\frac{1}{2}$ in (16.25 cm) $1\frac{1}{4}$ in (3.1 cm)

$4\frac{1}{4}$ in (10.8 cm)

$1\frac{1}{4}$ in (3.1 cm)

A

E F $5\frac{1}{2}$ in (14 cm)

B C

$1\frac{1}{2}$ in (3.8 cm) 3 in (7.6 cm)

D

STEP 1 Measure and cut the various pieces from a sheet of bond paper, as shown. Two additional pieces E and F are needed, as shown.

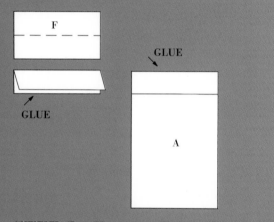

F

GLUE

GLUE

A

STEP 2 Use piece F to make nose ballast. Lay flat in a horizontal direction and valley fold horizontally. Glue halves together. Then glue to piece A, as shown.

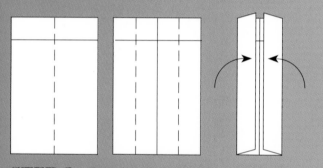

STEP 3 Lay piece A flat in a vertical direction. To make the fuselage, fold in half vertically using a valley fold. Unfold. Then valley fold each side so that outer edges meet center crease, as shown.

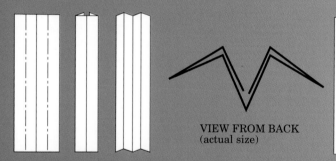

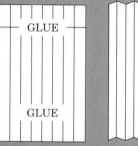

VIEW FROM BACK
(actual size)

STEP 4 Fold each side again using a mountain fold, so that outer edges meet center crease at back. Then adjust folds so that paper looks like an upside-down W, as shown.

GLUE

GLUE

STEP 5 Unfold fuselage completely. Refold applying glue to all contacting surfaces, as shown. Make sure fuselage is straight.

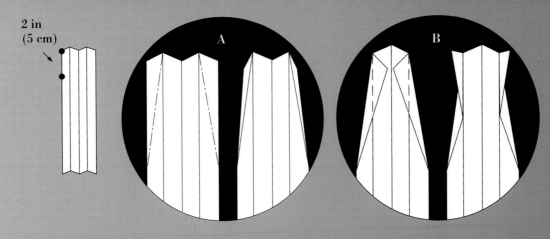

2 in
(5 cm)

A

B

STEP 6 On each side, measure from top (front of fuselage), mark, and mountain fold along broken lines, as shown in enlarged view A. Then flip over fuselage. On each side, valley fold triangle along broken lines, matching fold line to existing crease, as shown in enlarged view B.

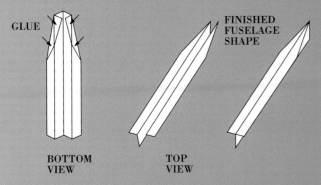

GLUE

FINISHED
FUSELAGE
SHAPE

BOTTOM
VIEW

TOP
VIEW

STEP 7 Glue triangles. Hold in place until glue sets. It is important that the fuselage stays straight. Do not glue nose yet.

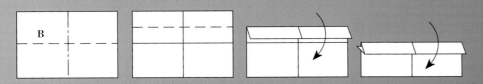

B

STEP 8 Lay piece B horizontally to make the wings. Fold in half horizontally, using a valley fold. Unfold. Fold in half vertically, using a mountain fold. Unfold. Then valley fold so that upper edge meets center crease. Fold over again along original center crease.

STEP 7   Unfold completely. Refold applying glue to no more than 1 in (2.5) cm) from outer tips, as shown. The folded over part is the bottom of the leading edge (front) of the wings.

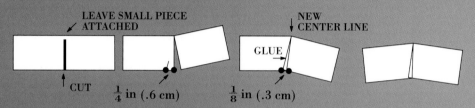

LEAVE SMALL PIECE ATTACHED

NEW CENTER LINE

GLUE

CUT $\frac{1}{4}$ in (.6 cm) $\frac{1}{8}$ in (.3 cm)

STEP 8   To taper wings, cut along center heavy line from trailing edge (back), leaving a small piece attached at the leading edge. Then measure and make a mark on trailing edge, as shown. Align pieces to the mark. Glue. Measure and draw a new center line.

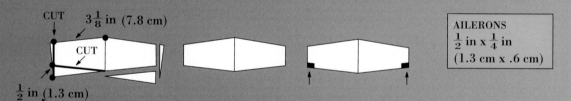

CUT $3\frac{1}{8}$ in (7.8 cm)

CUT

$\frac{1}{2}$ in (1.3 cm)

AILERONS
$\frac{1}{2}$ in x $\frac{1}{4}$ in
(1.3 cm x .6 cm)

STEP 9   On each side, measure and cut, as indicated by heavy lines. On the trailing edges of wingtips, make ailerons.

$\frac{5}{8}$ in (1.6 cm)

C

ELEVATORS
$\frac{3}{4}$ in x $\frac{1}{4}$ in
(1.9 cm x .6 cm)

STEP 10   Use piece C to make the horizontal tail. Valley fold in half vertically. Unfold. On each side, measure from center crease, as shown, and mountain fold. On each side, measure and mountain fold leading edge along broken lines. Glue. Make elevators on trailing edges.

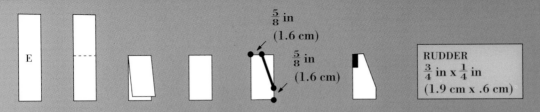

$\frac{5}{8}$ in
(1.6 cm)

$\frac{5}{8}$ in
(1.6 cm)

RUDDER
$\frac{3}{4}$ in x $\frac{1}{4}$ in
(1.9 cm x .6 cm)

STEP 11   Lay piece E vertically to make the vertical tail. Valley fold in
half horizontally and glue halves together. Measure and cut along heavy line,
as shown. Make rudder on trailing edge.

CANOPY (type 1)
$1\frac{1}{4}$ in x $8\frac{1}{2}$ in (3.1 cm x 21.7 cm)
Top point $1\frac{1}{2}$ in (3.8 cm)
Back is straight

SLIT $1\frac{1}{4}$ in (3.2 cm)

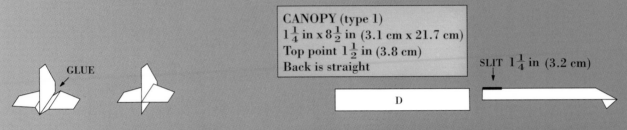

GLUE

D

STEP 12   Finish the tail. Apply glue to
inside of horizontal tail and slide vertical
tail in place, aligning at trailing edge.

STEP 13   Use piece D to make the canopy
(see p 28). Make slit in the back of canopy.

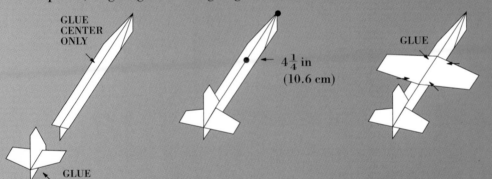

GLUE
CENTER
ONLY

$4\frac{1}{4}$ in
(10.6 cm)

GLUE

GLUE

STEP 14   Apply glue to inside center only of fuselage. Then apply glue and slide tail into
fuselage, aligning at trailing edge. Measure from front and mark for wing position. Glue wings
to fuselage.

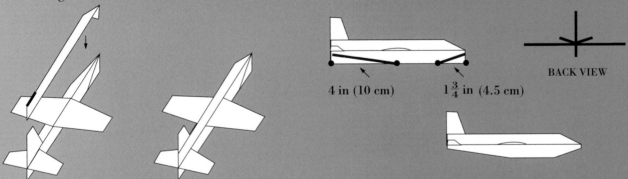

4 in (10 cm)

$1\frac{3}{4}$ in (4.5 cm)

BACK VIEW

STEP 15   Apply glue to inside back of canopy and front tab of canopy. Insert tab into fuselage.
The vertical tail fits into slit. Align at nose. To finish, measure and cut front and back of fuselage
along heavy diagonal lines, as shown. Adjust dihedral (upward slanting of wings and tail).

Mirage 2000

HISTORICAL INFORMATION

High-speed flight became common after World War II, and wings that swept back came into widespread use because of their efficiency at high speed. Filling in the space between the wingtips of swept-back wings resulted in the formation of triangle shaped wings (delta wings). Delta wings are very stable in flight and are good for supersonic flight. One of their first successful applications was in the early 1950s on the experimental Fairey Delta that exceeded 1000 mph. Two other supersonic planes of the 1950s were the General Dynamics F106 Delta Dart and the Dassault-Breguet Mirage 3. The Mirage has been upgraded several times and is still being built as the Mirage 2000. This paper airplane is modeled on it.

Technical Information

Delta Wings: The triangle shape of these wings has a unique affect on the air flowing over their upper surfaces. The air flows diagonally towards the fuselage. Like swept-back wings, delta wings prevent the buildup of the pressure ridge created by high speed flight. In addition, the shape lends added stability, and most delta wing airplanes need no additional horizontal stabilizers. However, because they are so stable, some fighter planes have surfaces added to make them less stable and more maneuverable. Delta wings can operate at much greater angles of attack before the air flowing over the top surfaces becomes turbulent and the wings stall.

42

Making the Mirage

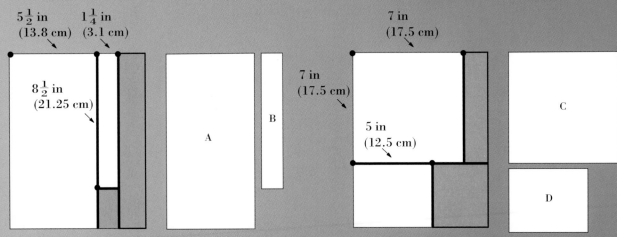

$5\frac{1}{2}$ in (13.8 cm) $1\frac{1}{4}$ in (3.1 cm)   7 in (17.5 cm)

$8\frac{1}{2}$ in (21.25 cm)

7 in (17.5 cm)

5 in (12.5 cm)

A

B

C

D

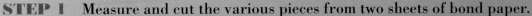

STEP 1   Measure and cut the various pieces from two sheets of bond paper.

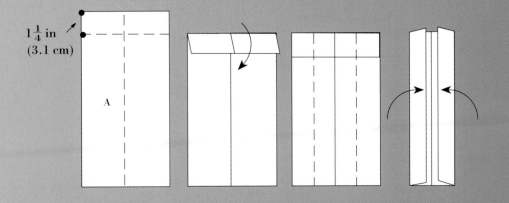

$1\frac{1}{4}$ in (3.1 cm)

A

STEP 2   Lay piece A vertically to make the fuselage. Fold in half vertically using a valley fold. Unfold. Measure from top and valley fold, as shown. Valley fold each side so that outer edges meet center crease, as shown.

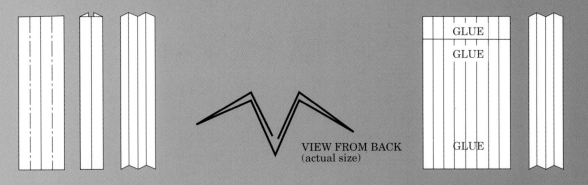

VIEW FROM BACK (actual size)

GLUE

GLUE

GLUE

STEP 3   Fold each side again using a mountain fold, so that outer edges meet center crease at back. Then adjust folds so that paper looks like an upside-down W, as shown.

STEP 4   Unfold fuselage completely. Refold, applying glue to contacting surfaces, as shown. Make sure fuselage is straight.

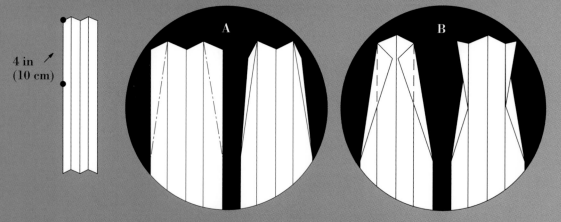

4 in
(10 cm)

STEP 5   On each side, measure from top (front of fuselage), mark, and mountain fold along broken lines, as shown in enlarged view A. Then flip over fuselage. On each side, valley fold triangle along broken lines, matching fold line to existing crease, as shown in enlarged view B.

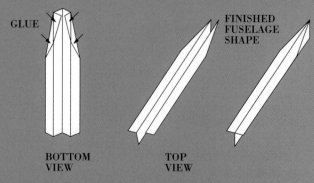

GLUE

FINISHED
FUSELAGE
SHAPE

BOTTOM
VIEW

TOP
VIEW

STEP 6   Glue triangles. Hold in place until glue sets. It is important that the fuselage stays straight. Do not glue nose yet.

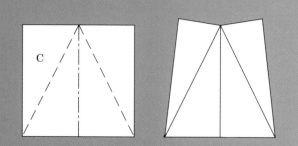

C

STEP 7   Use piece C to make the wings. Mountain fold in half vertically. Unfold. Draw a line from the top center to the lower corners and valley fold along lines, as shown. Unfold.

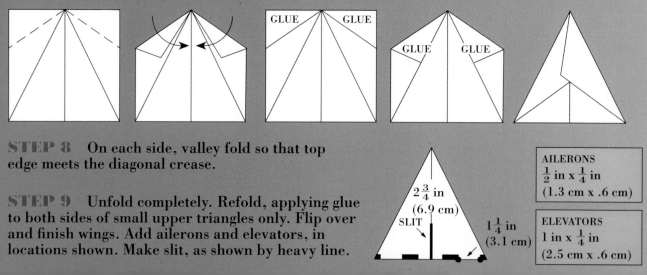

GLUE   GLUE

GLUE   GLUE

STEP 8   On each side, valley fold so that top edge meets the diagonal crease.

STEP 9   Unfold completely. Refold, applying glue to both sides of small upper triangles only. Flip over and finish wings. Add ailerons and elevators, in locations shown. Make slit, as shown by heavy line.

$2\frac{3}{4}$ in
(6.9 cm)

SLIT

$1\frac{1}{4}$ in
(3.1 cm)

AILERONS
$\frac{1}{2}$ in x $\frac{1}{4}$ in
(1.3 cm x .6 cm)

ELEVATORS
1 in x $\frac{1}{4}$ in
(2.5 cm x .6 cm)

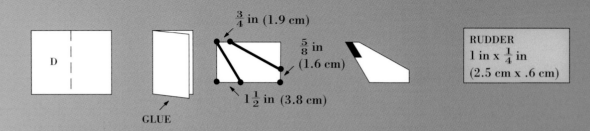

RUDDER
1 in x $\frac{1}{4}$ in
(2.5 cm x .6 cm)

STEP 10 Lay piece D horizontally to make the vertical tail. Valley fold in half vertically. Glue halves together. Turn, as shown, measure, mark, and cut along heavy lines. Make rudder on trailing edge, as shown.

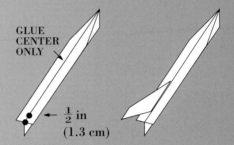

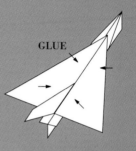

STEP 11 Apply glue to inside center only of fuselage. Measure from back of fuselage and mark, as shown. Then apply glue and slide tail into fuselage, aligning at mark.

STEP 12 Apply glue and attach wings to fuselage, slipping around vertical tail. Align trailing edge at the mark.

CANOPY (type 1)
$1\frac{1}{4}$ in x $8\frac{1}{2}$ in (3.1 cm x 21.7 cm)
Top point 3 in (7.5 cm)
Back $\frac{3}{8}$ in (1 cm)

STEP 13 Use piece B to make canopy (see p 28). Make a slit at center back of canopy.

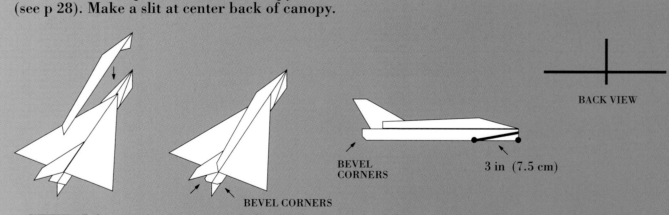

STEP 14 Apply glue to inside back of canopy and front tab of canopy. Insert tab into fuselage. The vertical tail fits into slit. Align at nose. Measure and cut front of fuselage along heavy diagonal line, as shown. To finish, bevel all corners on fuselage back, as shown.

Lifting Body

HISTORICAL INFORMATION

In the 1960s experiments were conducted into designing airplanes with flattened and widened fuselages so that these became lift-producing. This allowed for much smaller wings. Among these planes was the American built X20 Dyna-Soar. Others were the Soviet built Cosmos series of planes, that were actually rocketed into space. All the lifting-body research planes were used to study high speed gliding (therefore the word "soar" in the X20 name). The information gathered was used primarily in developing space vehicles. This paper airplane is modeled on the lifting-body research planes.

Technical Information

Lifting Bodies: The lifting-body research airplanes were not intended for operational use. They were used to demonstrate that wedge-shaped airplanes with very stubby wings could actually fly. Having small wings is important in an airplane that is to be rocketed into space orbit at high speed. Large wings could not stand the stress and would rip off. The angle of attack is very important in the flight of these planes, and is greater than in most airplanes. Because their wings are so small, these planes are roll-unstable. Some experimental planes rocked back and forth wildly in flight. This problem was eventually solved. One successful application of lifting-body research is the Space Shuttle. On its return from space orbit, the shuttle is the world's heaviest and fastest glider.

Making the Lifting Body

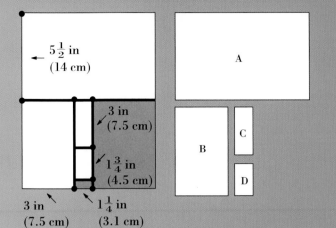

$5\frac{1}{2}$ in
(14 cm)

3 in
(7.5 cm)

$1\frac{3}{4}$ in
(4.5 cm)

3 in
(7.5 cm)

$1\frac{1}{4}$ in
(3.1 cm)

A

B

C

D

STEP 1   Measure and cut the various pieces from a sheet of bond paper, as shown.

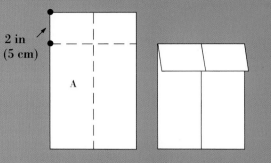

2 in
(5 cm)

A

STEP 2   Lay piece A flat in a vertical direction. To make the fuselage, fold in half vertically using a valley fold. Unfold. Measure from top and valley fold, as shown.

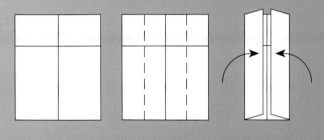

STEP 3   Valley fold each side so that outer edges meet center crease, as shown.

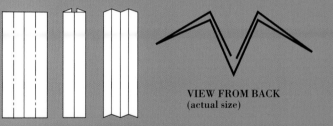

VIEW FROM BACK
(actual size)

STEP 4   Fold each side again using a mountain fold, so that outer edges meet center crease at back. Then adjust folds so that paper looks like an upside-down W, as shown.

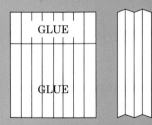

GLUE

GLUE

STEP 5   Unfold fuselage completely. Refold applying glue to all contacting surfaces, as shown. Make sure fuselage is straight.

2 in
(5 cm)

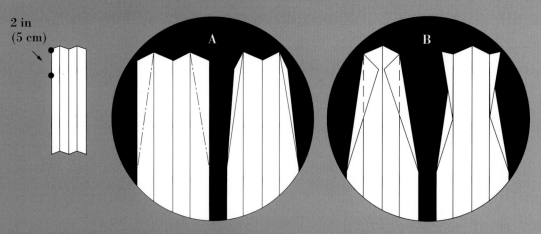

A

B

STEP 6 On each side, measure from top (front of fuselage), mark, and mountain fold along broken lines, as shown in enlarged view A. Then flip over fuselage. On each side, valley fold triangle along broken lines, matching fold line to existing crease, as shown in enlarged view B.

GLUE

FINISHED
FUSELAGE
SHAPE

BOTTOM
VIEW

TOP
VIEW

STEP 7 Glue triangles. Hold in place until glue sets. It is important that the fuselage stays straight. Do not glue nose yet.

B

STEP 8 Use piece B to make the wings. Lay paper flat in a horizontal direction. Mountain fold in half vertically. Unfold. Then fold each side diagonally so that upper edges meet center crease. Unfold.

RUDDERS	AILERONS	ELEVATORS
$\frac{3}{8}$ in x $\frac{1}{4}$ in	$\frac{3}{8}$ in x $\frac{1}{4}$ in	$\frac{3}{8}$ in x $\frac{1}{4}$ in
(1 cm x .6 cm)	(1 cm x .6 cm)	(1 cm x .6 cm)

GLUE

$1\frac{1}{2}$ in
(3.8 cm)

$1\frac{1}{8}$ in (2.8 cm)

SLIT

$1\frac{1}{4}$ in (3.1 cm)

STEP 9 On each side, valley fold diagonally so that outer edge meets previously made diagonal crease. Then apply glue to upper tip only and refold along original diagonal creases. Flip wings over. On each side, measure and valley fold wingtips to make vertical tails.

STEP 10 Make a slit at the center back of wings, as shown. Make rudders, ailerons, and elevators in locations shown.

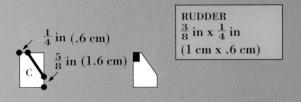

$\frac{1}{4}$ in (.6 cm)

$\frac{5}{8}$ in (1.6 cm)

C

RUDDER
$\frac{3}{8}$ in x $\frac{1}{4}$ in
(1 cm x .6 cm)

CANOPY (type 2)
$1\frac{1}{4}$ in x 3 in (3.1 cm x 7.5 cm)
Top point 2 in (5 cm)

D

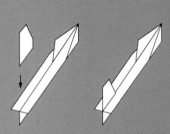

STEP 11 Use piece C to make a center vertical tail. Measure and cut, as shown. Make rudder in location shown.

STEP 12 Use piece D to make the canopy. (See p 28).

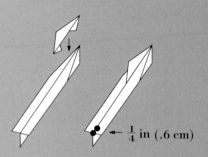

← $\frac{1}{4}$ in (.6 cm)

STEP 13 Applying glue to inside of fuselage at the nose end, insert tabs on the bottom of canopy, aligning at front. Measure from back of fuselage and mark wing position.

STEP 14 Applying glue to bottom part of vertical tail, insert into back of fuselage, aligning at back edge.

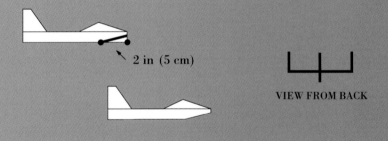

2 in (5 cm)

VIEW FROM BACK

STEP 15 Glue wings to fuselage. Align trailing (back) edge to the mark so that slit fits around center vertical tail.

STEP 16 Measure from front of fuselage and cut nose, as shown by heavy diagonal line. Adjust vertical tails to be vertical.

Glider

HISTORICAL INFORMATION

While Wilber Wright was mainly interested in powered flight, his brother Orville experimented with gliders. Both types of flight continued to be developed. By the time World War II ended much had been learned about good aerodynamic performance. During the 1950s and 60s the design of gliders was greatly improved as builders produced low-drag gliders with highly efficient wings. With long soaring flights now possible, Orville's dream of sustained motorless flight was fulfilled. In Europe, Germany became well known for its gliders. In the USA, the Schweizer brothers of New York built good training gliders that did much to promote gliding in North America. Soaring became a popular sport the world over. This paper airplane is modeled on gliders.

Technical Information

Aspect Ratio: Wings that are short, like the ones found on the X1 and the Lifting Body, have a low aspect ratio. Wings that are long and slender have a high aspect ratio. Wings with a high aspect ratio produce more lift for the amount of drag they create. This makes them suitable for gliders, where the smallest amount of drag possible is best. Today's gliders are very efficient. They soar like the eagles. From an altitude of 6000 ft (1800 m) some of them can fly about 60 nautical miles forward without any additional lift. To gain altitude, pilots usually take advantage of columns of rising air. (This is air that has been warmed by the ground on a sunny day, making it lighter and consequently making it rise.) Some glider pilots have remained airborne for more than ten hours and flown distances of more than 1000 nautical miles without landing. They have reached altitudes of more than 40,000 ft (12,000 m). Because the columns of rising air are invisible, it takes skill, and sometimes luck, to find and stay in them. Many countries have national gliding competitions where the best pilots demonstrate their skills.

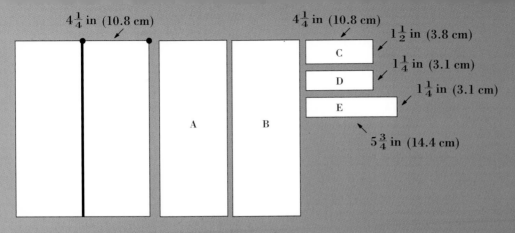

A   B

4¼ in (10.8 cm)   4¼ in (10.8 cm)   1½ in (3.8 cm)

C

1¼ in (3.1 cm)

D

1¼ in (3.1 cm)

E

5¾ in (14.4 cm)

STEP 1 Measure and cut a sheet of bond paper, as shown. Three additional pieces are needed, as shown.

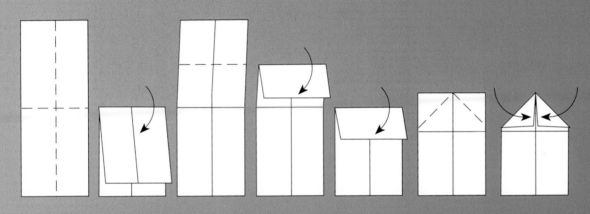

STEP 2 To make the fuselage, fold piece A in half vertically using a valley fold. Unfold. Valley fold in half horizontally. Unfold. Then valley fold so that upper edge meets horizontal crease. Refold original horizontal crease. Then on each side, valley fold diagonally so that top edge meets center crease.

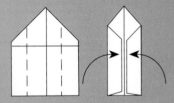

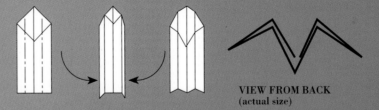

VIEW FROM BACK
(actual size)

STEP 3 Valley fold each side so that outer edges meet center crease, as shown.

STEP 4 Fold again using a mountain fold, so that outer edges meet center crease at back. Then adjust folds so that paper looks like an upside-down W, as shown.

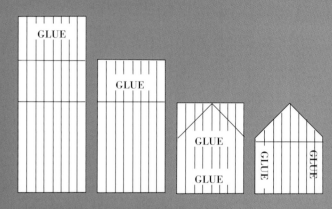

STEP 5 Unfold fuselage completely. Refold, applying glue to contacting surfaces, as shown. Make sure fuselage is straight.

STEP 6 Glue center of fuselage, leaving 1 in (2.5 cm) at the nose and 1 in (2.5 cm) at the tail end unglued. Round corners at nose end.

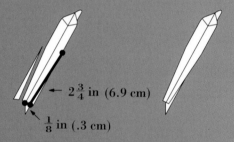

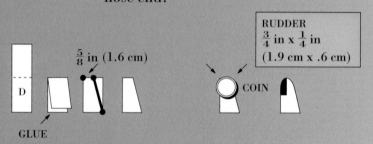

RUDDER
$\frac{3}{4}$ in x $\frac{1}{4}$ in
(1.9 cm x .6 cm)

STEP 7 On each side, measure and cut fuselage back, as shown by heavy lines.

STEP 8 Lay piece D vertically to make the vertical tail. Valley fold in half horizontally. Glue halves together. Measure and cut leading edge along heavy line, as shown. Trace around a coin and cut out to round corners (see p 26). On trailing edge, make rudder.

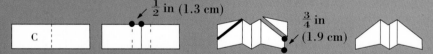

STEP 9 Use piece C to make the horizontal tail. Valley fold in half vertically. Unfold. On each side, measure from center crease, as shown, and mountain fold. On each side, measure and cut leading edges along heavy lines, as shown.

ELEVATORS
$1\frac{1}{4}$ in x $\frac{1}{4}$ in
(3.1 cm x .6 cm)

STEP 10 Trace around a coin and cut out to make all the corners rounded (see p 26). On trailing edges, make elevators.

STEP 11 Apply glue to inside of horizontal tail and insert vertical tail, aligning trailing edges.

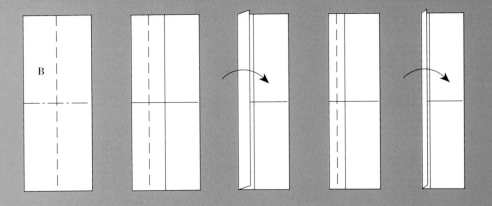

STEP 12 Use piece B to make the wings. Fold in half horizontally, using a mountain fold. Unfold. Fold in half vertically, using a valley fold. Unfold. Then valley fold so that outer edge meets center crease. Fold same side again so that outer edge again meets center crease. Refold original horizontal center crease.

GLUE   GLUE

STEP 13 Unfold completely. On each side, draw and cut diagonally along heavy lines, as shown. Refold. Apply glue before refolding original horizontal center crease only. The folded over part is the bottom of the leading edge (front) of the wings. These slender wings are quite fragile. When they are completed, make sure they are not twisted.

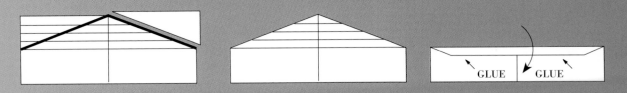

$\frac{7}{8}$ in
(2.3 cm)

COIN

STEP 14 Measure and cut trailing edge (back) of wings, as shown by heavy lines. Then trace around a coin and cut out to make rounded corners at both leading edges and trailing edges, as shown (see p 26).

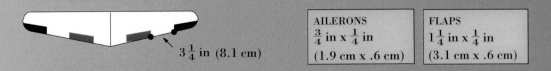

$3\frac{1}{4}$ in (8.1 cm)

AILERONS	FLAPS
$\frac{3}{4}$ in x $\frac{1}{4}$ in	$1\frac{1}{4}$ in x $\frac{1}{4}$ in
(1.9 cm x .6 cm)	(3.1 cm x .6 cm)

STEP 15 At wingtips on trailing edges, make ailerons. Then make secondary control surfaces (flaps), in locations shown.

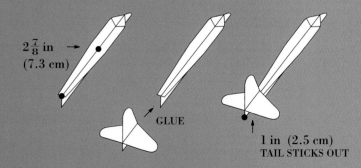

$2\frac{7}{8}$ in
(7.3 cm) →

GLUE

1 in (2.5 cm)
TAIL STICKS OUT

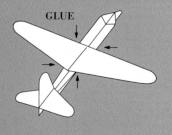

GLUE

STEP 16 Measure from back of fuselage and mark position of leading edge (front) of wing. Apply glue and slide tail into back of fuselage.

STEP 17 At the mark, attach wings to fuselage.

CANOPY (type 1)
$1\frac{1}{4}$ in x $5\frac{3}{4}$ in (3.1 cm x 14.6 cm)
Top point 1 in (2.5 cm)
Back $\frac{1}{4}$ in (.6 cm)

E

SLIT $\frac{3}{4}$ in (1.9 cm)

← ROUNDED TOP POINT

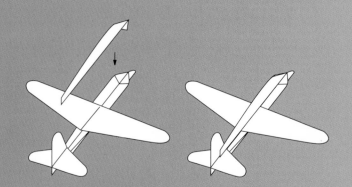

STEP 18 Make the canopy, using piece E (see p 28). Make a slit at the center back, as shown. Round the top point slightly.

STEP 19 Apply glue to inside back and front tab of canopy. Insert tab into fuselage, sliding vertical tail into slit. Align at nose.

VIEW FROM BACK

STEP 20 Measure and cut back of fuselage along heavy diagonal line, as shown. Adjust dihedral (upward slanting of wings and tail), as shown.

F16 Falcon

HISTORICAL INFORMATION

In the early 1970s the General Dynamics F16 was an experimental airplane used to test new lightweight materials and computer technology. Since then it has become one of the most maneuverable and versatile fighter planes ever made, and is used for a wide range of military tasks. It can be found in the air forces of at least ten countries. Its ailerons, elevators, and rudder, as well as navigation and weapons systems, are controlled by computer. The plane has modified delta wings with a conventional tail. For added stability it has a pair of canted (slanted) ventral fins beneath the horizontal stabilizers. It is commonly called the "Falcon". This paper airplane in modeled on the F16.

Technical Information

The F16 has a flattened fuselage, something like a lifting body. While the wings of this plane are basically triangular, they attach to the fuselage with extensions on the leading edges called strakes. They improve the flight characteristics of the plane at very low and very high speeds. In this paper model the flattened fuselage acts as part of the leading edge extensions. The F16 has a single turbojet engine with an afterburner and can fly twice the speed of sound at an altitude of 60,000 ft (18,000 m). Its air intake is situated in line with the canopy underneath the fuselage. The F16 has much improved fuel efficiency over older jet fighters. It has a missile rail at each wingtip, and can carry extra fuel tanks as well as a variety of armament under the wings. This makes it useful for both air-to-air and air-to-ground military operations. Besides its military role, this aircraft is also used as an aerial display plane at air shows.

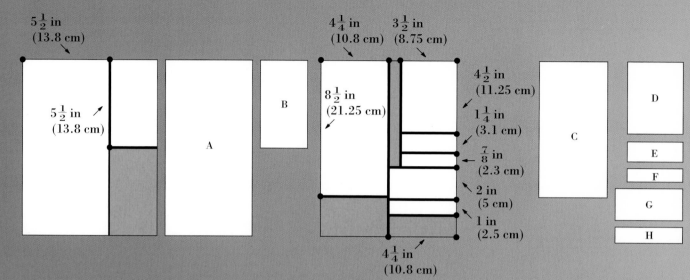

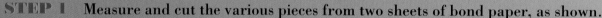

STEP 1 Measure and cut the various pieces from two sheets of bond paper, as shown.

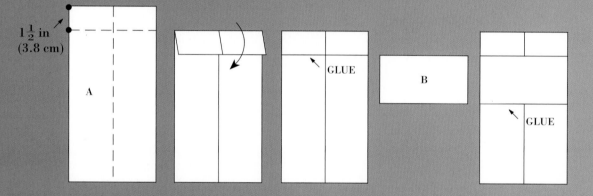

STEP 2 Lay piece A flat in a vertical direction. To make the fuselage, fold in half vertically using a valley fold. Unfold. Measure and valley fold horizontally, as shown. Glue this flap down. Then glue piece B in place, aligning against the glued-down flap, as shown.

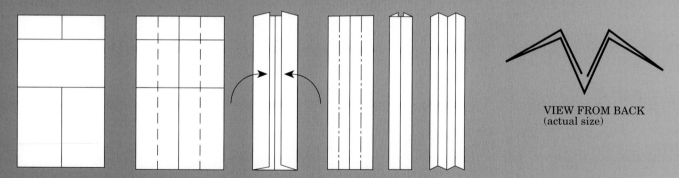

VIEW FROM BACK
(actual size)

STEP 3 Refold in half vertically using a valley fold. Unfold. Valley fold each side so that the outer edges meet center crease, as shown. Fold each side again using a mountain fold, so that outer edges meet center crease at back. Then adjust folds so that paper looks like an upside-down W, as shown.

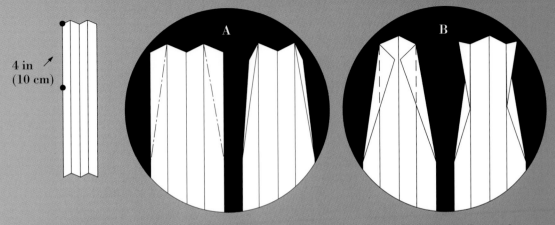

**4 in
(10 cm)**

A

B

STEP 4 On each side, measure from top (front of fuselage), mark, and mountain fold along broken lines, as shown in enlarged view A. Then flip over fuselage. On each side, valley fold triangle along broken lines, matching fold line to existing crease, as shown in enlarged view B.

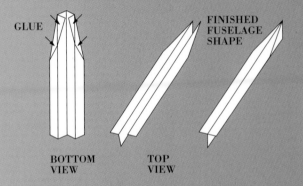

GLUE

BOTTOM
VIEW

TOP
VIEW

FINISHED
FUSELAGE
SHAPE

STEP 5 Glue triangles. Hold in place until glue sets. It is important that the fuselage stays straight. Do not glue nose yet.

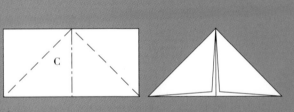

C

STEP 6 Use piece C to make the wings. Fold in half vertically, using a mountain fold. Unfold. On each side, valley fold diagonally so that top edge meets center crease, as shown.

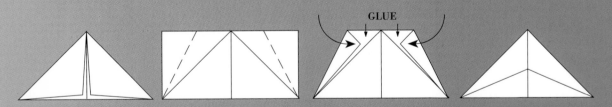

GLUE

STEP 7 Unfold diagonal folds. On each side, valley fold diagonally so that outer edges meet diagonal crease, as shown. Apply glue to small upper triangles only and refold original diagonal creases.

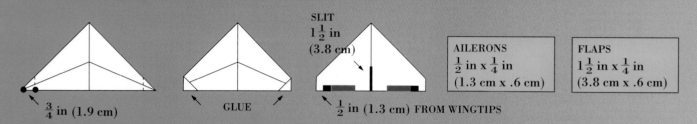

SLIT
$1\frac{1}{2}$ in (3.8 cm)

$\frac{3}{4}$ in (1.9 cm)

GLUE

$\frac{1}{2}$ in (1.3 cm) FROM WINGTIPS

AILERONS	FLAPS
$\frac{1}{2}$ in x $\frac{1}{4}$ in	$1\frac{1}{2}$ in x $\frac{1}{4}$ in
(1.3 cm x .6 cm)	(3.8 cm x .6 cm)

STEP 8 At each wingtip, measure and valley fold, as shown. Glue down the small triangles. Flip over and make ailerons and flaps in locations shown. At the trailing edge, make a slit along the center crease.

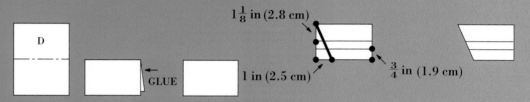

D

GLUE

$1\frac{1}{8}$ in (2.8 cm)

1 in (2.5 cm)

$\frac{3}{4}$ in (1.9 cm)

STEP 9 Mountain fold piece D in half horizontally to make the vertical tail. Glue halves together.

STEP 10 Measure and draw lines, as shown. Cut diagonally, as shown by heavy lines.

ELEVATORS
$1\frac{3}{8}$ in x $\frac{3}{8}$ in
(3.5 cm x 1 cm)

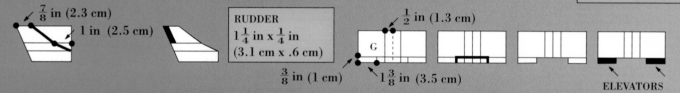

$\frac{7}{8}$ in (2.3 cm)

1 in (2.5 cm)

RUDDER
$1\frac{1}{4}$ in x $\frac{1}{4}$ in
(3.1 cm x .6 cm)

$\frac{3}{8}$ in (1 cm)

$\frac{1}{2}$ in (1.3 cm)

G

$1\frac{3}{8}$ in (3.5 cm)

ELEVATORS

STEP 11 Measure and draw additional lines to make leading edge, as shown. Cut diagonally, as shown by heavy lines. Add rudder.

STEP 12 Use piece G to make horizontal tail. Valley fold in half vertically. Unfold. On each side, measure and draw lines. To make elevators, cut out piece, as shown by heavy lines.

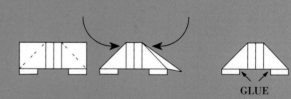

GLUE

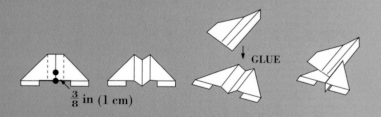

GLUE

$\frac{3}{8}$ in (1 cm)

STEP 13 On each side, mountain fold diagonally so that upper edge meets vertical crease, as shown. Glue.

STEP 14 Measure from back and make a mark. On each side, mountain fold along lines, as shown. Apply glue to inside of horizontal tail and isert vertical tail, aligning trailing edge (back) to the mark.

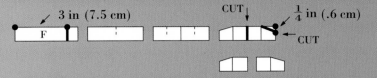

3 in (7.5 cm)   F

CUT   ¼ in (.6 cm)   CUT

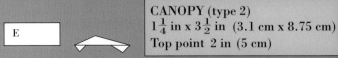

E

CANOPY (type 2)
$1\frac{1}{4}$ in x $3\frac{1}{2}$ in (3.1 cm x 8.75 cm)
Top point 2 in (5 cm)

STEP 15 Cut piece F to size for the ventral fins, as shown. Mountain fold in half vertically. Unfold. On each side, mountain fold in half vertically so that outer edge meets center crease. Unfold. On each side, measure and cut, as shown by heavy line. Then cut in two along center crease.

STEP 16 Use piece E to make the canopy. (See p 28.)

STEP 17 Measure from front of fuselage and make marks for positioning the leading edges of canopy at I, wings at J, ventral fins at K.

FROM FRONT OF FUSELAGE

I $\frac{3}{8}$ in (1 cm)

J $3\frac{3}{4}$ in (9.5 cm)

K $7\frac{5}{8}$ in (19.4 cm)

STEP 18 Apply glue to inside of nose and the small tabs on the bottom of the canopy. Slide canopy in place. Hold until glue sets. Next, glue ventral fins in place. Then glue wings in place overlapping ventral fins, as shown.

GLUE

GLUE

GLUE

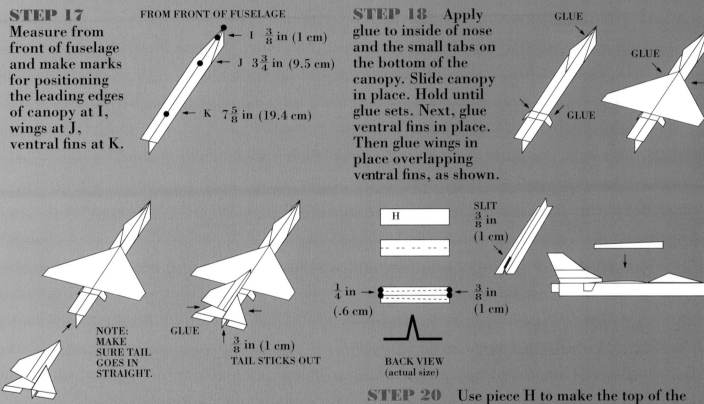

NOTE: MAKE SURE TAIL GOES IN STRAIGHT.

GLUE

$\frac{3}{8}$ in (1 cm)
TAIL STICKS OUT

H

SLIT
$\frac{3}{8}$ in
(1 cm)

$\frac{1}{4}$ in → (.6 cm)   ← $\frac{3}{8}$ in (1 cm)

BACK VIEW
(actual size)

STEP 19 Apply glue and slide tail into fuselage. The tail sticks out of the back end of fuselage, with the vertical tail sliding into slit in the wings.

STEP 20 Use piece H to make the top of the fuselage. Mountain fold in half horizontally. Unfold. On each side of crease, measure and valley fold, as shown. Make slit. Glue onto top of fuselage, as shown. The vertical tail slides into slit. Fit the front snuggly over back of canopy.

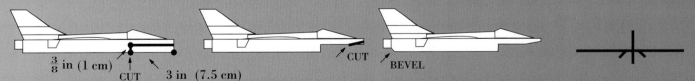

$\frac{3}{8}$ in (1 cm)   CUT   3 in (7.5 cm)   CUT   BEVEL

STEP 21 Measure and cut nose, as shown. First cut a rectangular notch, then cut the tip diagonally to give final shape to the nose. Bevel back of fuselage. This plane has no dihedral. Ventral fins are canted (slanted) 45°.

F18 Hornet

HISTORICAL INFORMATION

The F16 was used as a land-based fighter aircraft but there was no equivalent sea-based fighter. Therefore the F18 was built in the early 1980s as a medium sized multi-task maneuverable military aircraft capable of both sea and land operations. This plane is commonly called the "Hornet." It has tapered wings and a conventional horizontal tail, but with two canted (tilted) vertical tails located between the wings and horizontal tail. The F18 is used by the USA, Canada, Australia, and Spain. This paper airplane is modeled on the F18.

Technical Information

The F18 is constructed mostly of aluminum, with parts of its wings and other surfaces made of composites. It has two afterburning turbojet engines that can propel it at almost twice the speed of sound when traveling at high altitude. This airplane is both a fighter and an attack plane, and it can be fitted with a wide variety of armament for both air-to-air and air-to-ground military tasks. Like the F16, it has a missile rail at each wingtip, with space under the wings for other armament and extra fuel tanks. Besides its military role, this plane is also used as an aerial display airplane at air shows.

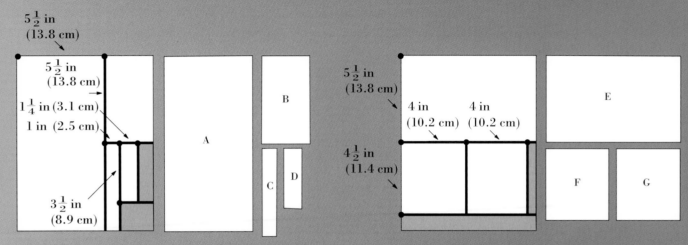

$5\frac{1}{2}$ in
(13.8 cm)

$5\frac{1}{2}$ in
(13.8 cm)

$1\frac{1}{4}$ in (3.1 cm)

1 in (2.5 cm)

A

B

C   D

$3\frac{1}{2}$ in
(8.9 cm)

$5\frac{1}{2}$ in
(13.8 cm)

4 in
(10.2 cm)

4 in
(10.2 cm)

$4\frac{1}{2}$ in
(11.4 cm)

E

F   G

STEP 1   Measure and cut the various pieces from two sheets of bond paper.

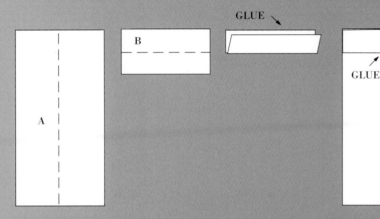

GLUE

B

A

GLUE

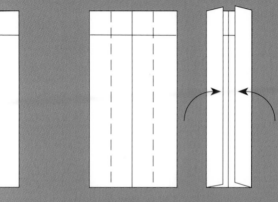

STEP 2   Use piece A to make the fuselage. Fold in half vertically using a valley fold. Unfold. Then valley fold piece B in half horizontally to make nose ballast. Glue halves together. Glue B to A, aligning top edges, as shown.

STEP 3   Valley fold so that outer edges meet center crease.

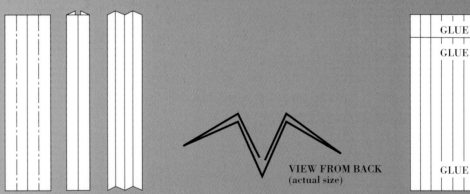

VIEW FROM BACK
(actual size)

GLUE

GLUE

GLUE

STEP 4   Fold each side again using a mountain fold, so that outer edges meet center crease at back. Then adjust folds so that paper looks like an upside-down W, as shown.

STEP 5   Unfold fuselage completely. Refold applying glue to contacting surfaces, as shown. Make sure fuselage is straight.

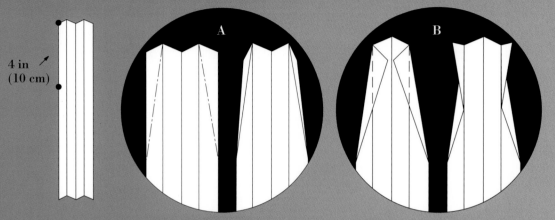

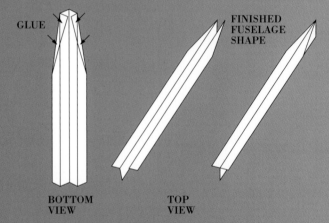

STEP 6 On each side, measure from top (front of fuselage), mark, and mountain fold along broken lines, as shown in enlarged view A. Then flip over fuselage. On each side, valley fold the triangle along the broken lines, matching fold line to existing crease, as shown in enlarged view B.

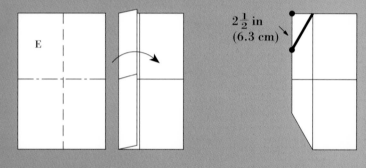

STEP 7 Glue triangles. Hold in place until glue sets. It is important that the fuselage stays straight. Do not glue nose yet.

STEP 8 Lay piece E in a vertical direction to make wings. Valley fold in half vertically. Unfold. Mountain fold in half horizontally. Valley fold so that one outer edge meets center crease, as shown. On each side of horizontal center crease , measure and cut diagonally, as shown by heavy line.

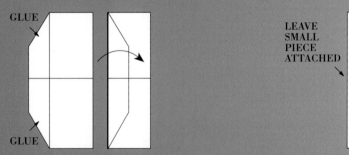

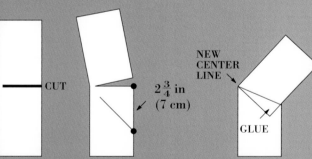

STEP 9 Apply glue to each diagonal side on top layer only, no more than 1 in (2.5 cm) from the diagonal edge. Refold along the original vertical center crease. The folded-over part is the bottom of the leading edge (front) of wings.

STEP 10 To taper wings, cut along center line from the trailing edge (back), leaving a small piece attached at the leading edge. Then measure and draw diagonal line, as shown. Align halves to the diagonal line. Glue. Draw new center line.

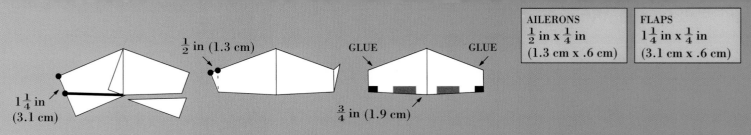

STEP 11 On each side, measure and cut trailing edge, as shown by heavy line. Then on each side, measure and mountain fold wingtips. Glue. Make ailerons and flaps in locations shown.

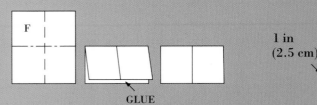

STEP 12 Lay piece F flat in a vertical direction to make the horizontal tail. Valley fold in half vertically. Unfold. Mountain fold in half horizontally. Glue halves together.

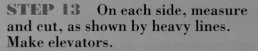

ELEVATORS
$1\frac{1}{4}$ in x $\frac{3}{8}$ in
(3.1 cm x 1 cm)

STEP 13 On each side, measure and cut, as shown by heavy lines. Make elevators.

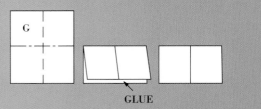

STEP 14 Lay piece G flat in a vertical direction to make the twin vertical tails. Valley fold in half vertically. Unfold. Mountain fold in half horizontally. Glue halves together.

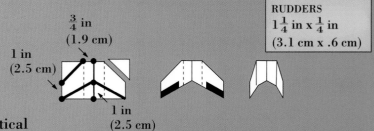

RUDDERS
$1\frac{1}{4}$ in x $\frac{1}{4}$ in
(3.1 cm x .6 cm)

STEP 15 On each side, measure and cut, as shown by heavy lines. Make a rudder on each vertical tail. On each side, valley fold, as shown.

CANOPY (type 2)
$1\frac{1}{4}$ in x $3\frac{1}{2}$ in (3.1 cm x 8.9 cm)
Top point $2\frac{1}{2}$ in (6.4 cm)

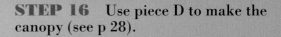

STEP 16 Use piece D to make the canopy (see p 28).

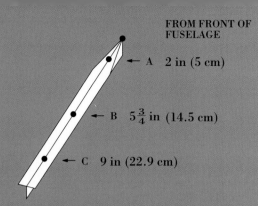

← A   2 in (5 cm)

← B $5\frac{3}{4}$ in (14.5 cm)

← C   9 in (22.9 cm)

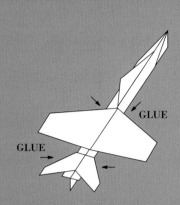

GLUE

GLUE

STEP 17   Measure from front of fuselage, as shown, and make mark A for positioning the front of the canopy, mark B for positioning leading edge of the wings, and mark C for positioning leading edge of the horizontal tail.

STEP 18   Apply glue to the inside of the nose and the small triangles on the bottom of the canopy. Position canopy on the fuselage at mark A. Hold until glue sets. Glue wings and horizontal tail in place, making sure they are centered and at right angles to the fuselage.

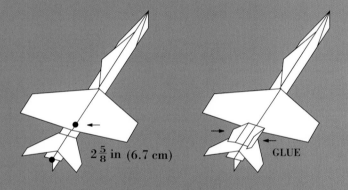

$2\frac{5}{8}$ in (6.7 cm)

GLUE

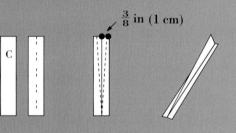

$\frac{3}{8}$ in (1 cm)

C

STEP 19   Measure from back of fuselage, as shown, and make a mark for positioning the twin vertical tails. Glue vertical tails in place, making sure they are centered and parallel to the fuselage.

STEP 20   Lay piece C in a vertical direction to make the fuselage top. Mountain fold in half vertically. Unfold. On each side, measure and valley fold. Adjust shape, as shown.

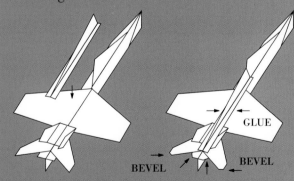

GLUE

BEVEL   BEVEL

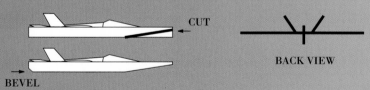

CUT

BEVEL

BACK VIEW

STEP 21   Glue piece C onto the fuselage, making sure it fits snugly against the canopy. Bevel the trailing edges of the elevators.

STEP 22   Measure and cut nose diagonally, as shown by heavy line. Bevel all corners of the back of the fuselage. Wings and horizontal tail are level. Adjust angles of the canted (tilted) vertical tails, as shown.

747 Jumbo

HISTORICAL INFORMATION

The first jet-powered airliner was the deHavilland Comet built in the 1950s. As more and more people realized the comfort of jet travel, bigger airplanes were needed to carry them. The Boeing 747 was first built in 1968. It is one of the largest passenger-carrying airplanes in the world. It is longer than the distance flown by the Wright brothers (120 ft or 36 m)) in their first powered flight. The "Jumbo Jet" is used to carry passengers and cargo across the continents and the oceans of the world. This paper airplane is modeled on the 747.

Technical Information

The Boeing 747 is a big airplane. From nose to tail it measures 230 ft (69 m). The distance from wingtip to wingtip is 195 ft (58.5 m). Its tail is 64 ft (19 m) high, higher than a five storey building. When it is fully loaded with fuel, passengers, and cargo, it weighs 800,000 lb (360,000 kg), and carries 500 passengers or 270,000 lb (121,500 kg) of cargo. Once it reaches high altitude, it cruises at 600 mph (960 km/h). This makes it ideal for use on long-distance passenger routes. Its service ceiling is 40,000 ft (12,000 m) above the ground. Its maximum range is 6000 miles (9600 km), allowing it to fly one fourth of the distance around the earth without refueling. The plane is propelled by four 50,000 lb thrust turbofan jet engines.

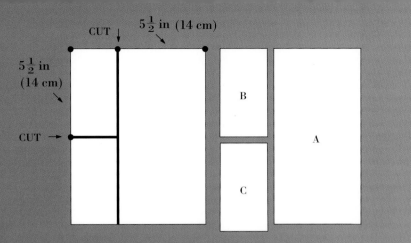

STEP 1 Measure and cut three pieces from a sheet of bond paper, as shown.

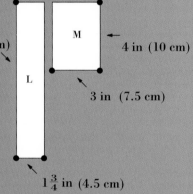

STEP 2 Valley fold a second sheet of bond paper in half vertically. Then measure and cut two pieces, as shown.

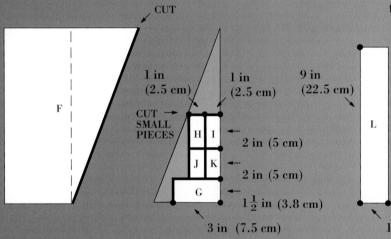

STEP 3 Valley fold a third sheet of bond paper in half vertically. Then measure and cut six pieces, as shown.

STEP 4 Measure and cut two additional pieces, as shown.

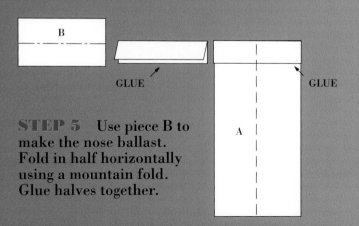

STEP 5 Use piece B to make the nose ballast. Fold in half horizontally using a mountain fold. Glue halves together.

STEP 6 Use piece A to make the fuselage. Glue ballast to the top of fuselage, as shown. Fold in half vertically using a valley fold. Unfold.

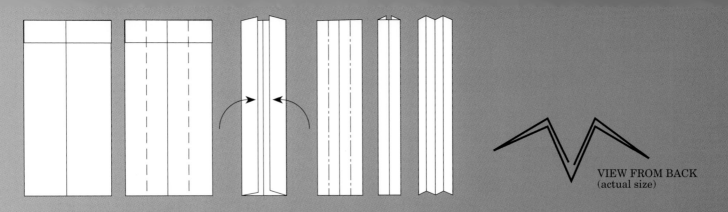

STEP 7   Valley fold each side so that outer edges meet center crease, as shown.

STEP 8   Fold each side again using a mountain fold, so that outer edges meet center crease at back. Then adjust folds so that paper looks like an upside-down W, as shown.

VIEW FROM BACK
(actual size)

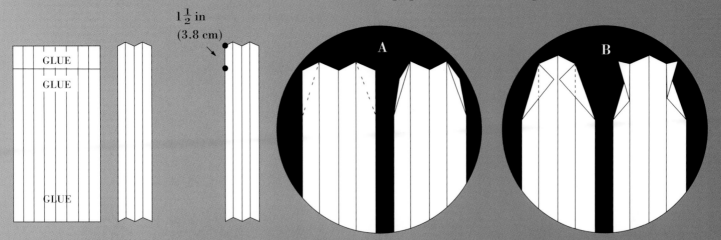

$1\frac{1}{2}$ in
(3.8 cm)

GLUE

GLUE

GLUE

A

B

STEP 9   Unfold fuselage completely. Refold applying glue to contacting surfaces, as shown. Make sure fuselage is straight.

STEP 10   On each side, measure from top (front of fuselage), mark, and mountain fold along broken lines, as shown in enlarged view A. Then flip over fuselage. On each side, valley fold triangle along broken lines, matching fold line to existing crease, as shown in enlarged view B.

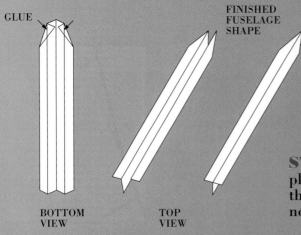

GLUE

FINISHED
FUSELAGE
SHAPE

BOTTOM
VIEW

TOP
VIEW

STEP 11   Glue triangles. Hold in place until glue sets. It is important that the fuselage stays straight. Do not glue nose yet.

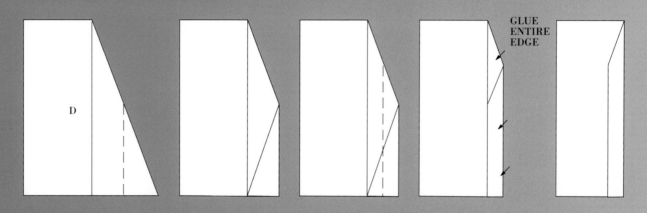

STEP 12 Lay piece D vertically to make the right wing. Valley fold vertically so that bottom outer edge meets center crease. Valley fold vertically again so that outer edge meets center crease. Apply glue. Then fold over again along original vertical center crease.

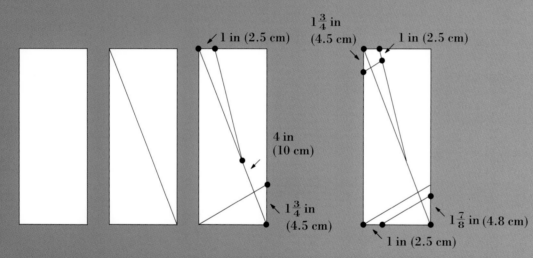

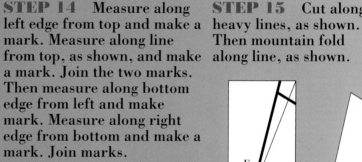

STEP 13 Flip over, with folded-over edge to the LEFT. Draw diagonal line from upper left to lower right corners. Measure along line from bottom and make a mark. Measure along top edge from left and mark. Join the two marks. Then measure along right edge from bottom and mark. Join this point with the bottom left corner.

STEP 14 Measure along left edge from top and make a mark. Measure along line from top, as shown, and make a mark. Join the two marks. Then measure along bottom edge from left and make mark. Measure along right edge from bottom and make a mark. Join marks.

STEP 15 Cut along heavy lines, as shown. Then mountain fold along line, as shown.

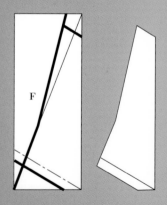

STEP 16 To make the left wing, repeat steps 12-15 using piece F, keeping the folded edge on the RIGHT and reversing the directions of the lines from left to right, as shown.

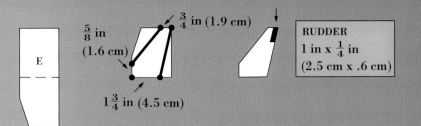

$\frac{5}{8}$ in
(1.6 cm)

$\frac{3}{4}$ in (1.9 cm)

$1\frac{3}{4}$ in (4.5 cm)

E

STEP 17 Lay piece E vertically to make the vertical tail. Valley fold in half horizontally and glue halves together. Then cut along heavy lines, as shown. Make rudder on trailing edge.

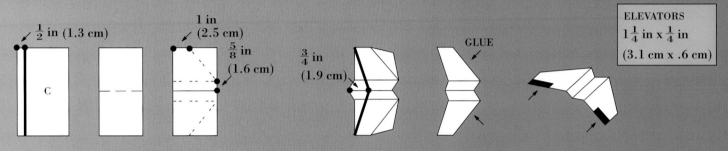

$\frac{1}{2}$ in (1.3 cm)

1 in
(2.5 cm)

$\frac{5}{8}$ in
(1.6 cm)

$\frac{3}{4}$ in
(1.9 cm)

GLUE

C

STEP 18 Lay piece C vertically to make the horizontal tail. Measure and cut to size. Valley fold in half horizontally. Unfold. On each side, measure from center crease, as shown, and mountain fold. On each side, measure and mountain fold leading edge along broken lines. Glue. Cut trailing edges and make elevators.

H I J K

G

GLUE

GLUE

STEP 19 Apply glue to inside of horizontal tail and insert vertical tail, aligning leading (front) edges.

STEP 20 Use piece G to make the canopy (see p 28). Use pieces H, I, J, and K to make the engines. Wrap each piece around a pencil vertically and glue.

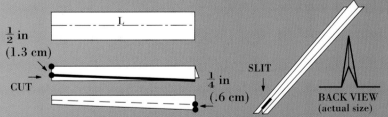

L

$\frac{1}{2}$ in
(1.3 cm)

CUT

$\frac{1}{4}$ in
(.6 cm)

SLIT

BACK VIEW
(actual size)

M

STEP 21 Use piece L to make the top of the fuselage. Mountain fold in half horizontally. Then, on each side, measure and valley fold to form piece, as shown. Cut a 1 in (2.5 cm) slit along center crease at narrow end.

STEP 22 Use piece M to make a spar (support) for the wings. Valley fold in half vertically. Unfold. Mountain fold in half horizontally. Unfold. Then valley fold vertically so that outer edge meets center crease. Fold over again along original vertical center crease.

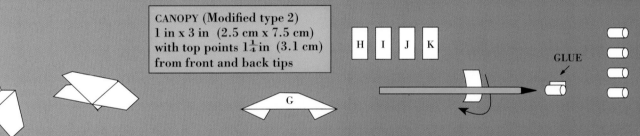
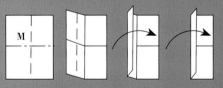

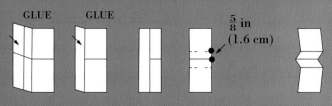

$\frac{5}{8}$ in (1.6 cm)

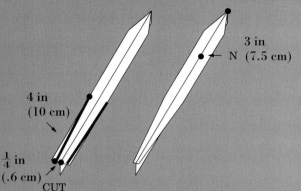

3 in (7.5 cm)   N

4 in (10 cm)

$\frac{1}{4}$ in (.6 cm)   CUT

STEP 23   Unfold spar completely. Refold, applying glue to contacting surfaces. Flip over. On each side of center crease, measure and mountain fold, as shown. Folded over edge is the front.

STEP 24   Measure back of fuselage and cut, as shown. Then measure from front and make mark for positioning leading edge of wings at N.

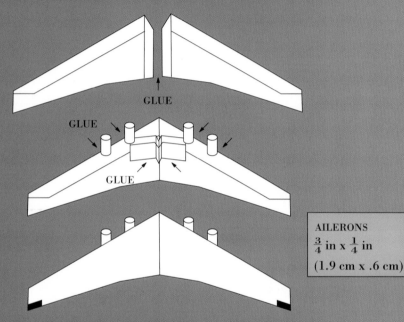

GLUE

GLUE

GLUE

AILERONS
$\frac{3}{4}$ in x $\frac{1}{4}$ in
(1.9 cm x .6 cm)

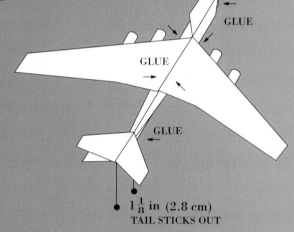

GLUE

GLUE

GLUE

$1\frac{1}{8}$ in (2.8 cm)
TAIL STICKS OUT

STEP 25   With wings upside down, glue halves together. Glue spar to wings. Glue engines to wings in approximate positions shown (they stick out $\frac{1}{2}$ in (1.3 cm)). Flip over. On trailing edges, make ailerons.

STEP 26   Apply glue to inside of fuselage, the small triangles on the bottom of canopy, and the center bottom of wings. Slide canopy tabs into fuselage aligning with front tip. Immediately slide wings in place. Then apply glue and slide tail into back of fuselage. Hold until glue sets.

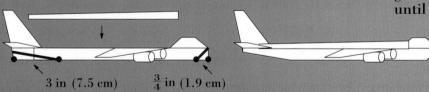

3 in (7.5 cm) $\frac{3}{4}$ in (1.9 cm)

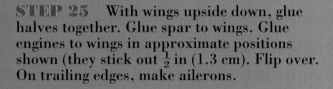

BACK VIEW

STEP 27   Measure and cut nose and tail ends diagonally along heavy lines, as shown. Glue L onto top of fuselage, as shown, fitting snuggly against back of canopy, with vertical tail through the slit. Adjust dihedral (upward slanting of wings and tail), as shown.

FSW Concept

HISTORICAL INFORMATION

Airplane builders are always trying to make planes that are more suited to special tasks. In the 1980s a new shape of airplane appeared. Grumman introduced the X29 forward swept wing (FSW) experimental airplane, using new composite materials that were very light and strong. Such a design was impossible to build with traditional materials. The advantages of sweeping the wings forward instead of backward allow for maneuverability and high angle of attack flight — desirable qualities for military application. This paper airplane is modeled on a forward swept wing aircraft that has not yet been built. This concept, designed by Grumman, is being considered for possible future development.

Technical Information

A future fighter will have to operate over a wide range of speeds, be very maneuverable, and be fuel efficient. It will have to be able to land in very small spaces. Forward swept wings combined with strakes (extensions of the leading edges near the fuselage) will improve the flight characteristics of the plane at very low and very high speeds. However, having no horizontal tail makes the plane sensitive to correct balance, and computers will aid in control. The light weight of composites, the lack of a horizontal tail, and better engines will allow improved fuel efficiency. The FSW Concept will probably have two turbojet engines and be able to fly at more than twice the speed of sound at high altitudes. Its air intakes will be part of the large strakes. The plane will have a missile rail at each wingtip, and be able to carry extra fuel tanks and a variety of armament under the wings. Like present day fighters, this craft will be used for both air-to-air and air-to-ground operations. Besides its military role, this airplane could be a good candidate for aerial display at air shows.

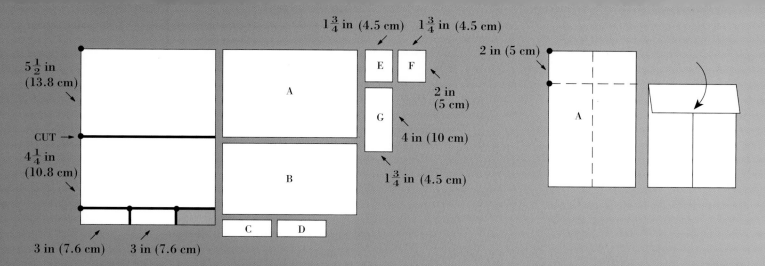

$5\frac{1}{2}$ in (13.8 cm)

CUT →

$4\frac{1}{4}$ in (10.8 cm)

3 in (7.6 cm)   3 in (7.6 cm)

A

B

C   D

$1\frac{3}{4}$ in (4.5 cm) $1\frac{3}{4}$ in (4.5 cm)

E   F

G

2 in (5 cm)

4 in (10 cm)

$1\frac{3}{4}$ in (4.5 cm)

2 in (5 cm)

A

STEP 1   Measure and cut pieces from a sheet of bond paper. Three additional pieces, E, F, and G are needed, as shown.

STEP 2   To make the fuselage, lay piece A in a vertical direction. Fold in half vertically, using a valley fold. Unfold. Measure from top and valley fold, as shown.

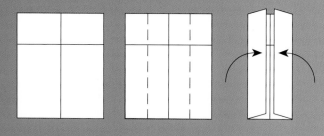

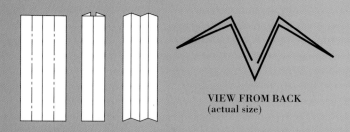

VIEW FROM BACK
(actual size)

STEP 3   Valley fold each side so that outer edges meet center crease, as shown.

STEP 4   Fold each side again using a mountain fold, so that outer edges meet center crease at back. Then adjust folds so that paper looks like an upside-down W, as shown.

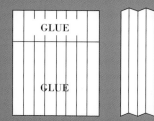

GLUE

GLUE

STEP 5   Unfold fuselage completely. Refold applying glue to all contacting surfaces, as shown. Make sure fuselage is straight.

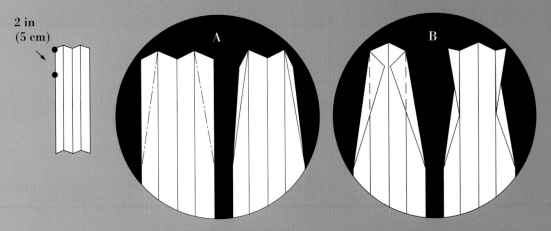

STEP 6   On each side, measure from top (front of fuselage), mark, and mountain fold along broken lines, as shown in enlarged view A. Then flip over fuselage. On each side, valley fold triangle along broken lines, matching fold line to existing crease, as shown in enlarged view B.

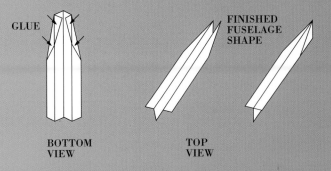

STEP 7   Glue triangles. Hold in place until glue sets. It is important that the fuselage stays straight. Do not glue nose yet.

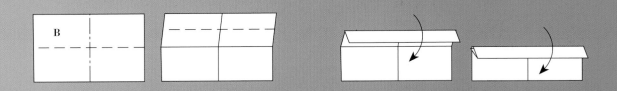

STEP 8   Use piece B to make the wings. Lay paper in a horizontal direction and fold in half vertically, using a mountain fold. Unfold. Valley fold in half horizontally. Unfold. Then valley fold horizontally so that top edge meets center crease. Fold over again along original center crease.

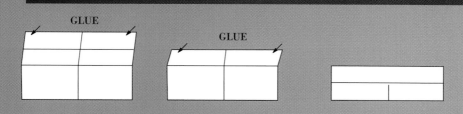

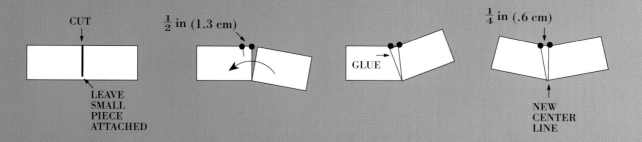

STEP 9 Unfold completely. Refold, applying glue to no more than 1 in (2.5 cm) from outer tips, as shown. The folded over part is the bottom of the leading edge (front) of the wings.

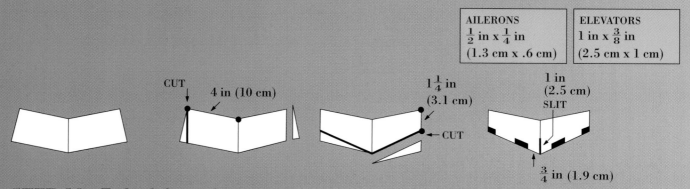

STEP 10 To sweep wings forward, cut along center line from the leading edge, leaving a small piece attached at the trailing edge (back). Then measure and make a mark on leading edge, as shown. Align pieces to the mark. Glue. Measure and draw new center line.

AILERONS	ELEVATORS
$\frac{1}{2}$ in x $\frac{1}{4}$ in	1 in x $\frac{3}{8}$ in
(1.3 cm x .6 cm)	(2.5 cm x 1 cm)

STEP 11 To finish forward swept wings, measure and cut wing tips along heavy lines. Then cut trailing edge along heavy lines, as shown. On trailing edges (back), make ailerons and elevators. From trailing edge, make a slit along center line, as shown.

RUDDERS
1 in x $\frac{3}{8}$ in
(2.5 cm x 1 cm)

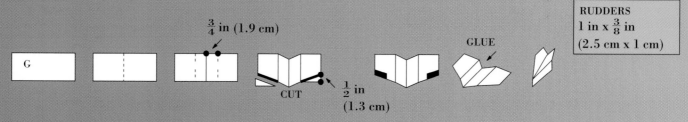

STEP 12 Use piece G to make the twin vertical tails. Lay paper in a horizontal direction. Valley fold in half vertically. Unfold. On each side, measure from center crease and mountain fold, as shown. Then measure and cut trailing edges, as shown by heavy lines. Make rudders. Glue center.

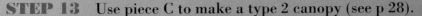

CANOPY (type 2)
$1\frac{1}{4}$ in x 3 in (3.1 cm x 7.5 cm)
Top point $1\frac{3}{4}$ in (4.5 cm)

STEP 13   Use piece C to make a type 2 canopy (see p 28).

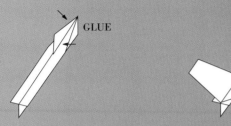

GLUE

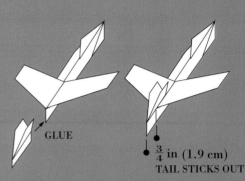

CUT →

GLUE

$\frac{3}{4}$ in (1.9 cm)
TAIL STICKS OUT

STEP 14   Apply glue to inside of nose and the small triangular tabs on the bottom of canopy. Slide tabs into fuselage, aligning canopy with the tip of the nose. Hold until glue sets.

STEP 15   Glue wings in place, aligning at the trailing (back) edge. Make sure they are centered and at right angles to the fuselage. Trim fuselage back flush with the wing trailing (back) edges.

STEP 16   Measure and mark along bottom of tail. Apply glue and slide tail into back of fuselage (and slit in the wings) to the mark.

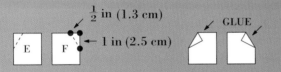

$\frac{1}{2}$ in (1.3 cm)

← 1 in (2.5 cm)

E   F

GLUE

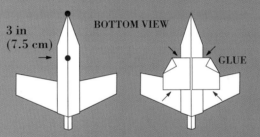

3 in
(7.5 cm)
→

BOTTOM VIEW

GLUE

STEP 17   Use pieces E and F to make the strakes. Lay pieces vertically side by side, as shown. Measure on outer left and right edges and valley fold diagonally, as shown. Glue.

STEP 18   Turn airplane over. Measure from front and mark, as shown. On each side, glue strakes in place, aligning inside corners to the mark.

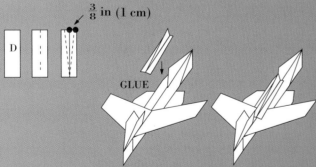

$\frac{3}{8}$ in (1 cm)

D

GLUE

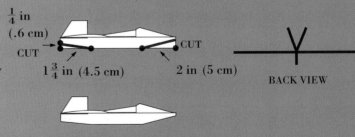

$\frac{1}{4}$ in
(.6 cm)
→
CUT

CUT

$1\frac{3}{4}$ in (4.5 cm)

CUT

2 in (5 cm)

BACK VIEW

STEP 19   Lay piece D in a vertical direction to make the fuselage top. Mountain fold in half vertically. Unfold. On each side, measure and valley fold. Adjust shape, as shown. Glue onto top of fuselage, as shown, fitting the front snuggly over back of canopy.

STEP 20   Measure and cut nose and tail diagonally, as shown by heavy lines. This plane has no dihedral. Twin tails are canted (tilted), as shown.

SST Concept

HISTORICAL INFORMATION

Flying faster than the speed of sound can only be done in areas of the world where no people live, because the loud sonic boom would break the windows in people's houses. Therefore, supersonic flights are undertaken only between cities across the world's oceans. However, the Sukoi and Gulfstream airplane companies are experimenting with planes of different shapes and sizes to see if they can reduce the intensity of the sonic boom. If the boom can be made quieter, supersonic air service between cities on the same continent or even in the same country would be possible. This paper airplane is modeled on a plane that has not yet been built. It is a concept of a future supersonic transport plane (SST).

Technical Information

The type of airplane being planned is probably small, carrying no more than ten passengers. This small size would be one way of making the boom produced in supersonic flight less damaging. The goal is to make the plane capable of traveling nearly twice the speed of sound. It will probably be built of lightweight composite materials and use computers for flight control. The plane's main wings will be delta wings with winglets at the tips. Winglets help direct the airflow over the wings. Canard wings for added control will also be used. This plane might be the business jet of the future.

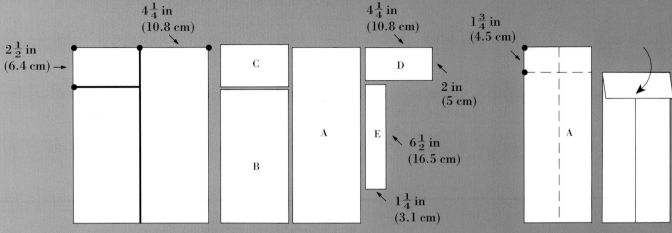

STEP 1 Measure and cut the various pieces from a sheet of bond paper. Two additional pieces, D and E, are needed, as shown.

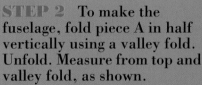

STEP 2 To make the fuselage, fold piece A in half vertically using a valley fold. Unfold. Measure from top and valley fold, as shown.

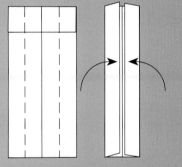

STEP 3 Valley fold each side so that outer edges meet center crease, as shown.

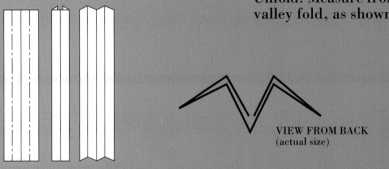

VIEW FROM BACK
(actual size)

STEP 4 Fold each side again using a mountain fold, so that outer edges meet center crease at back. Then adjust folds so that paper looks like an upside-down W, as shown.

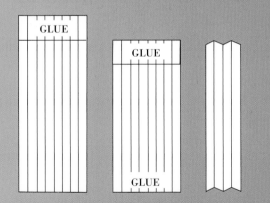

GLUE

GLUE

GLUE

STEP 5 Unfold fuselage completely. Refold applying glue to contacting surfaces, as shown. Make sure fuselage is straight.

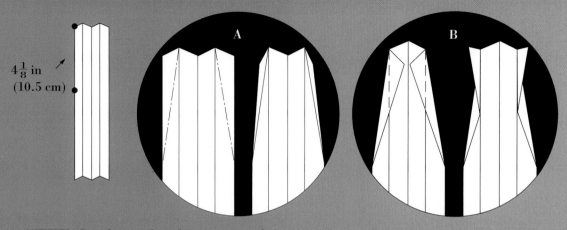

$4\frac{1}{8}$ in
(10.5 cm)

STEP 6 On each side, measure from top (front of fuselage), mark, and mountain fold along broken lines, as shown in enlarged view A. Then flip over fuselage. On each side, valley fold triangle along broken lines, matching fold line to existing crease, as shown in enlarged view B.

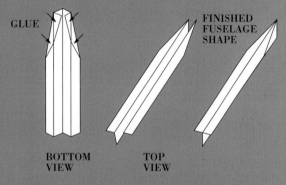

GLUE

FINISHED
FUSELAGE
SHAPE

BOTTOM
VIEW

TOP
VIEW

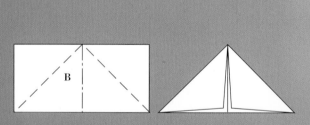

B

STEP 7 Glue triangles. Hold in place until glue sets. It is important that the fuselage stays straight. Do not glue nose yet.

STEP 8 Lay piece B flat in a horizontal direction to make the wings. Fold in half vertically, using a mountain fold. Unfold. On each side, valley fold diagonally so that top edge meets center crease, as shown.

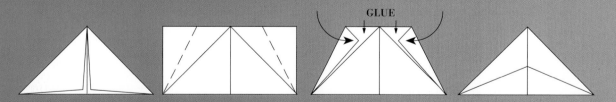

GLUE

STEP 9 Unfold diagonal folds. On each side, valley fold diagonally so that outer edges meet diagonal crease, as shown. Apply glue to small upper triangles only and refold original diagonal creases.

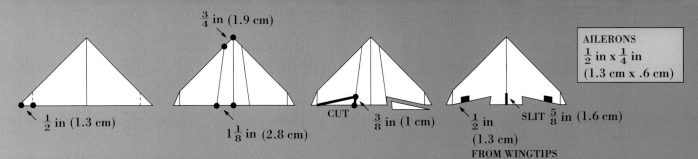

$\frac{3}{4}$ in (1.9 cm)

AILERONS
$\frac{1}{2}$ in x $\frac{1}{4}$ in
(1.3 cm x .6 cm)

$\frac{1}{2}$ in (1.3 cm)

$1\frac{1}{8}$ in (2.8 cm)

CUT $\frac{3}{8}$ in (1 cm)

$\frac{1}{2}$ in (1.3 cm) SLIT $\frac{5}{8}$ in (1.6 cm)
FROM WINGTIPS

STEP 10 Flip wings over. To make winglets, measure at each wingtip and valley fold, as shown. Then on each side, measure and draw lines, as shown. At the trailing edge, measure and cut, as shown by heavy lines. Make ailerons in locations shown. Measure and cut a slit in location shown.

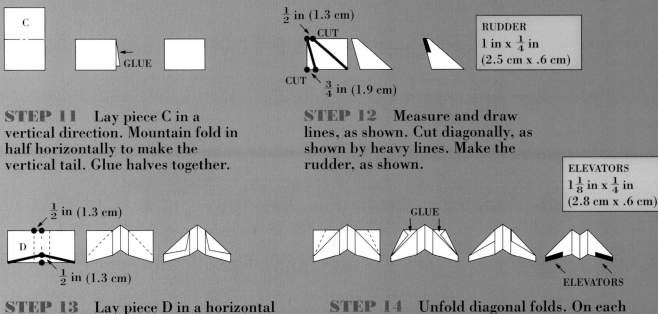

C

GLUE

$\frac{1}{2}$ in (1.3 cm)
CUT

CUT $\frac{3}{4}$ in (1.9 cm)

RUDDER
1 in x $\frac{1}{4}$ in
(2.5 cm x .6 cm)

STEP 11 Lay piece C in a vertical direction. Mountain fold in half horizontally to make the vertical tail. Glue halves together.

STEP 12 Measure and draw lines, as shown. Cut diagonally, as shown by heavy lines. Make the rudder, as shown.

ELEVATORS
$1\frac{1}{8}$ in x $\frac{1}{4}$ in
(2.8 cm x .6 cm)

$\frac{1}{2}$ in (1.3 cm)

D

$\frac{1}{2}$ in (1.3 cm)

GLUE

ELEVATORS

STEP 13 Lay piece D in a horizontal direction to make canard wings. Mountain fold in half vertically. Unfold. Measure from bottom along center crease and cut, as shown by heavy lines. On each side, measure and valley fold. Then on each side, fold diagonally so that top edge meets vertical crease.

STEP 14 Unfold diagonal folds. On each side, valley fold diagonally so that outer edges meet diagonal creases, as shown. Apply glue to small upper triangles only and refold original diagonal creases. Flip wings over and make elevators in locations shown.

CANOPY (type 1)
$1\frac{1}{4}$ in x $6\frac{1}{2}$ in (3.1 cm x 16.5 cm)
Top point $1\frac{3}{4}$ in (4.5 cm)
Back $\frac{3}{8}$ in (1 cm)

SLIT $\frac{5}{8}$ in (1.6 cm)

E

STEP 15 Use piece E to make a type 1 canopy (see p 28).

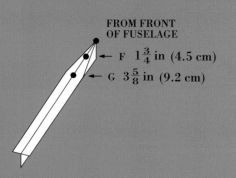

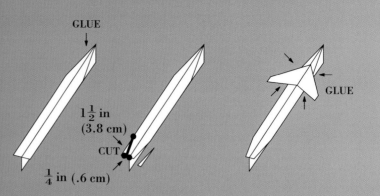

STEP 16   Measure from front of fuselage and make marks for positioning the leading edges of canard wings and canopy at F and main wings at G, as shown.

STEP 17   Apply glue to inside of nose, no more than 1 in (2.5 cm) from tip. Hold until glue sets. Then measure and cut back of fuselage, as shown. Glue canard wings in place. (Do not glue the inside center of the canard wings.)

STEP 18   Glue main wings in place, making sure they are centered and at right angles to the fuselage. Then measure from back of fuselage and mark.

STEP 19   Apply glue and slide vertical tail into back of fuselage so that trailing edge aligns with mark.

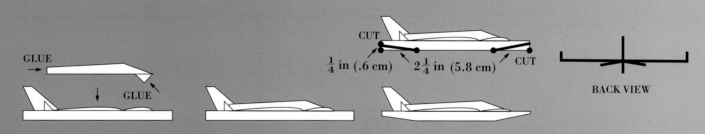

STEP 20   Apply glue to the tabs on the bottom of canopy and the inside back of the canopy. Slide tab into center of canard wings with the slit fitting around the vertical tail. Align canopy front with front of canard wings.

STEP 21   Measure and cut nose and tail, as shown by heavy lines. The wings of this airplane have no dihedral. Adjust winglets to a vertical position.

TAV Concept

HISTORICAL INFORMATION

We are living on the threshold of a new era in air travel. Already the space shuttle is blasting into space attached to a rocket and returning as an airplane for another mission. The next generation of space planes will take off under their own power from ordinary airport runways, fly into space, and return back to earth. They are called trans-atmospheric vehicles (TAV). Sometimes they are called hypersonic transports (HST). They will combine jet and rocket engines for propulsion and have stable delta wings (triangle shaped) integrated into the fuselage for lift in the lower atmosphere. They will look something like the ordinary "paper plane." One example is NASAs experimental X30. This paper airplane is modeled on such future space planes.

Technical Information

Trans-atmospheric vehicles will need powerful and complicated engines and fuel supplies if they are to fly from the ground up into space. It takes a great deal of energy to propel an airplane beyond the limits of the earth's atmosphere and go into space orbit at 22 times the speed of sound. For example, the space shuttle we have now uses over 1,000,000 lb (600,000 kg) of liquid oxygen and 300,000 lb (120,000 kg) of liquid hydrogen, which it burns in under ten minutes of flight. The fuel is carried in large external tanks, which are thrown away during each flight. Future TAVs will carry everything on-board, like a regular airplane. In addition to engines for very high altitude, they will also have engines that can burn fuel using oxygen from the atmosphere at lower altitudes. Only at very high altitudes, where there is not enough oxygen in the air to use, will they switch to an on-board supply of oxygen. Space planes of the future will use less fuel and carry much less oxygen. Such planes will be able to fly competely around the world in just a few hours.

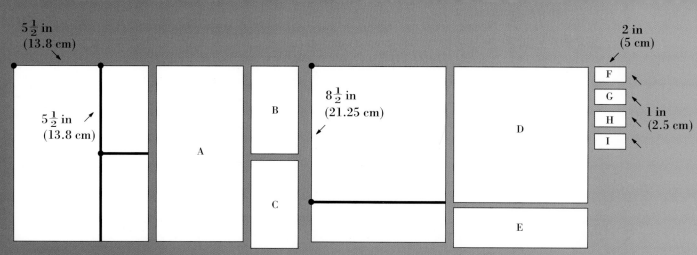

5½ in
(13.8 cm)

5½ in
(13.8 cm)

A

B

C

8½ in
(21.25 cm)

D

E

2 in
(5 cm)

F

G

H

I

1 in
(2.5 cm)

STEP 1 Measure and cut the various pieces from two sheets of bond paper. Four additional small pieces are needed, as shown.

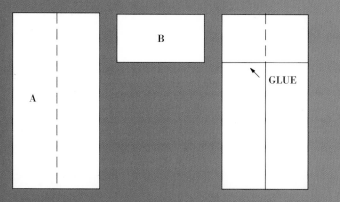

A

B

GLUE

STEP 2 Lay piece A flat in a vertical direction. To make the fuselage, fold in half vertically using a valley fold. Unfold. To make nose ballast glue piece B in place, aligning the top edges, as shown. Refold center crease. Unfold again.

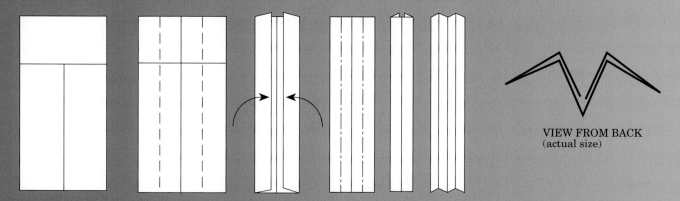

VIEW FROM BACK
(actual size)

STEP 3 Refold in half vertically using a valley fold. Unfold. Valley fold each side so that outer edges meet center crease, as shown. Fold each side again using a mountain fold, so that outer edges meet center crease at back. Then adjust folds so that paper looks like an upside-down W, as shown.

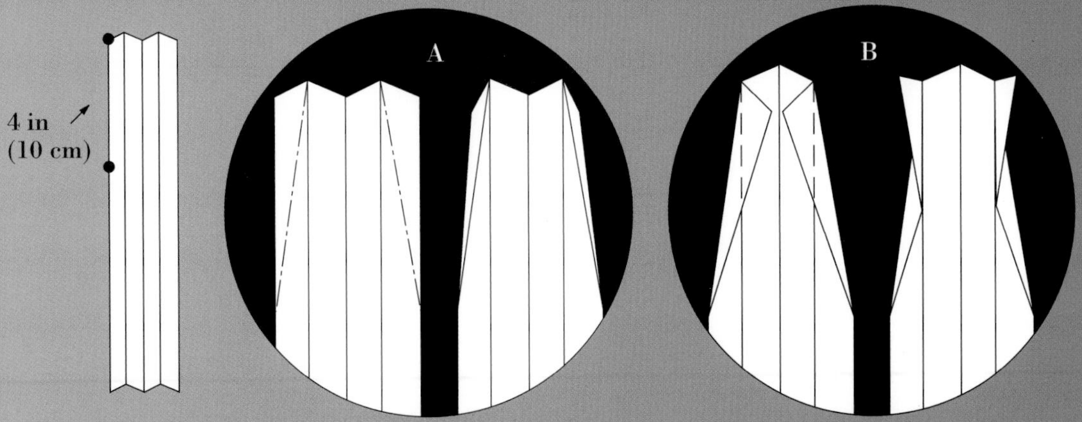

4 in
(10 cm)
A
B

STEP 4 On each side, measure from top (front of fuselage), mark, and mountain fold along broken lines, as shown in enlarged view A. Then flip over fuselage. On each side, valley fold the triangle along the broken lines, matching fold line to existing crease, as shown in enlarged view B.

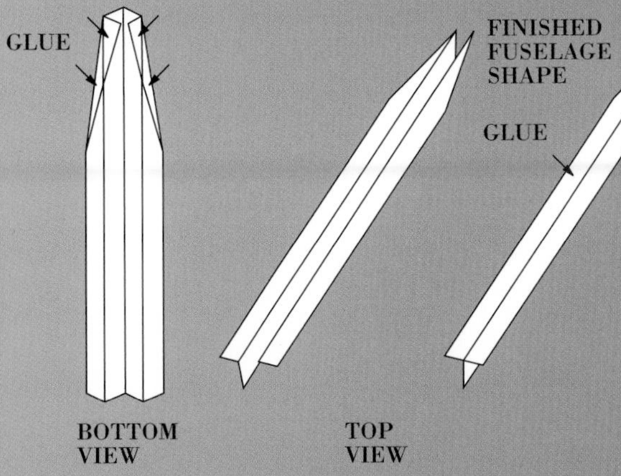

GLUE
FINISHED FUSELAGE SHAPE
GLUE
BOTTOM VIEW
TOP VIEW

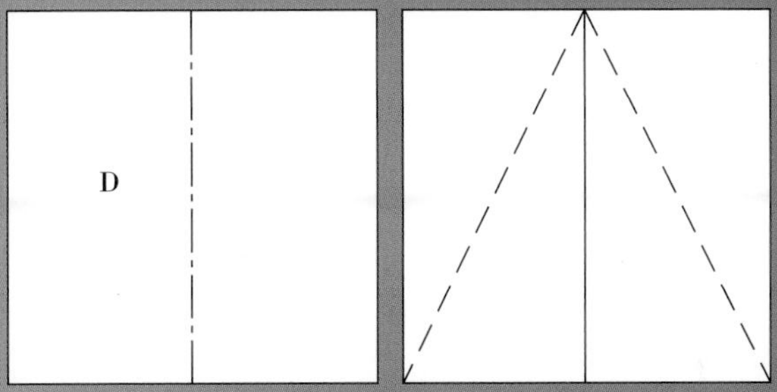

D

STEP 5 Glue triangles. Hold in place until glue sets. It is important that the fuselage stays straight. Glue fuselage in the middle only, leaving the nose and tail ends unglued.

STEP 6 Use piece D to make the wings. Mountain fold in half vertically. Unfold. Then on each side valley fold diagonally along a line running from the top center to the bottom corners. Unfold.

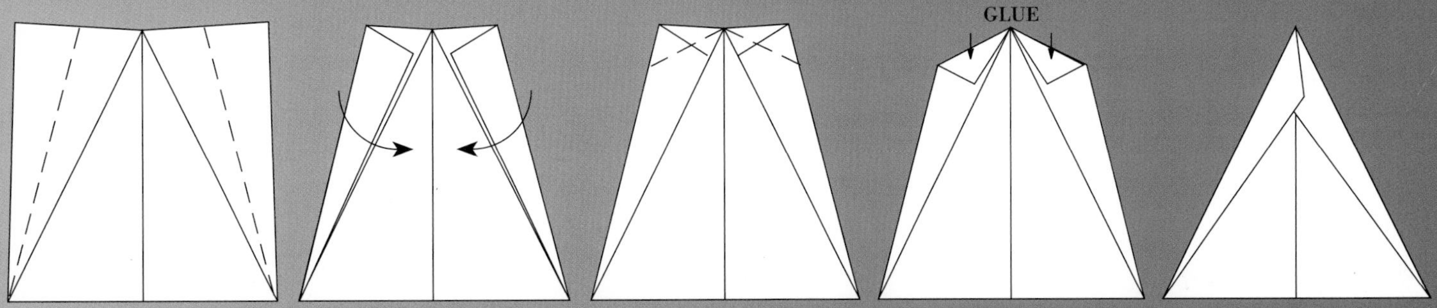

GLUE

STEP 7 On each side, valley fold diagonally so that outer edges meet diagonal crease, as shown. Then fold so that upper edges meet diagonal crease, as shown. Apply glue to the small upper triangles only and refold original diagonal creases.

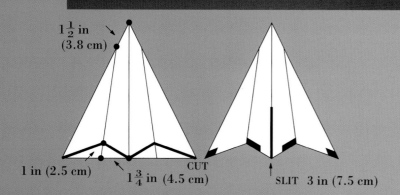

$1\frac{1}{2}$ in (3.8 cm)

1 in (2.5 cm)

$1\frac{3}{4}$ in (4.5 cm)

CUT

SLIT 3 in (7.5 cm)

STEP 8 Lay wings flat right side up. On each side measure from front tip and back center and draw lines, as shown. Then cut wings, as shown by heavy lines. Make elevators and ailerons in locations shown. At the trailing (back) edge, cut a slit along center crease, as shown.

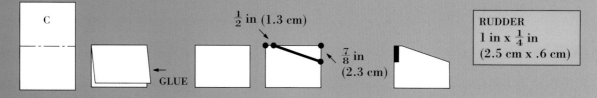

C

$\frac{1}{2}$ in (1.3 cm)

GLUE

$\frac{7}{8}$ in (2.3 cm)

RUDDER 1 in x $\frac{1}{4}$ in (2.5 cm x .6 cm)

STEP 9 Mountain fold piece C in half horizontally to make the vertical tail. Glue halves together. Measure and cut, as shown by heavy line. Make rudder, as shown.

SLIT $\frac{1}{2}$ in (1.3 cm)

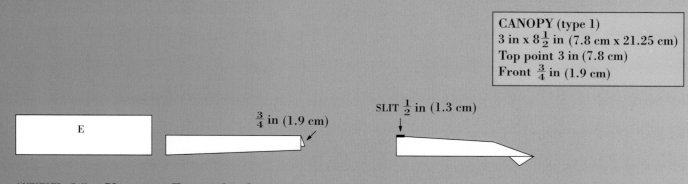

E

$\frac{3}{4}$ in (1.9 cm)

STEP 10 Use piece E to make the type 1 canopy (see p 28). Note that this canopy is lower at the front than at the back. Cut paper to size first.

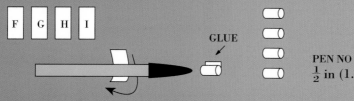

F G H I

GLUE

PEN NO THICKER THAN $\frac{1}{2}$ in (1.3 cm)

STEP 11 Use pieces F, G, H, and I to make the engines. Wrap paper around a felt pen vertically and glue.

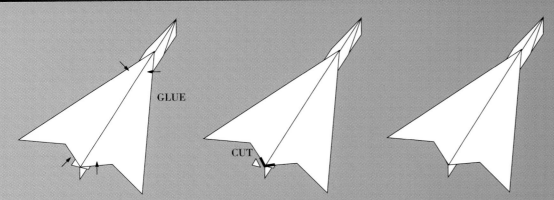

STEP 12 Glue wings to the fuselage, aligning trailing (back) edges. Make sure wings are centered and at right angles to the fuselage. Then trim back of fuselage to match wing trailing edges.

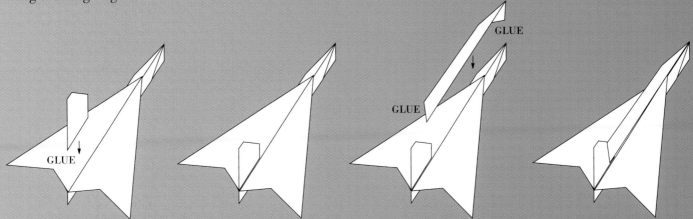

STEP 13 Apply glue and slide vertical tail into fuselage (and the slit in the wings). Align at trailing (back) edges. Apply glue to the lower front tab of the canopy and the inside back. Position canopy by inserting tab into nose end of the fuselage and slipping the back over the vertical tail.

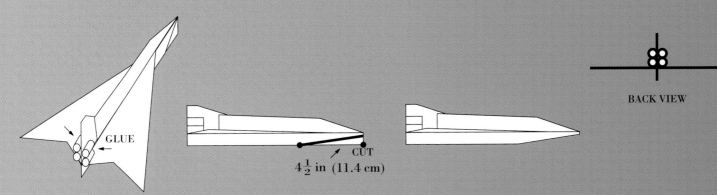

BACK VIEW

$4\frac{1}{2}$ in (11.4 cm)

STEP 14 Attach the engines by gluing them to the vertical tail, two on each side, one on top the other, as shown. Align to the trailing edge of the vertical tail.

STEP 15 Measure and cut nose diagonally, as shown by heavy line. This plane has no dihedral.

Decoration

The following pages contain a plan (top) view and an elevation (side) view of each of the paper airplanes contained in this book. They have window outlines, outlines of control surfaces, and other lines that help define each plane's shape, all of which add to an airplane's realism. Decorative patterns add interest.

The patterns can be copied, modified, or you can invent your own. A pattern such as a checkerboard or a camouflage that is shown on one plane can easily be applied to another airplane design. Use your imagination. What you see here are suggestions. Or you can build paper airplanes and leave them undecorated. You may wish to build undecorated trial planes first so you can master their construction and flight before you spend a lot of time on decoration.

It is easier to add decoration to the airplanes before they are completely assembled. Some advanced planning is needed. Once you have decided on the pattern or design you want for the plane, decorate the pieces as you cut and fold them. Try each piece for fit and mark it carefully as you go along. Armament can be added to military planes using toothpicks. Draw the decoration lines using a very fine black felt-tipped pen. Narrow colored markers are ideal for filling in. Avoid water-based markers because they wrinkle the paper too much. Stencils can be used to add numbers and letters.

See the photographed airplanes for ideas on color schemes. Some of the patterns may be different from those shown here.

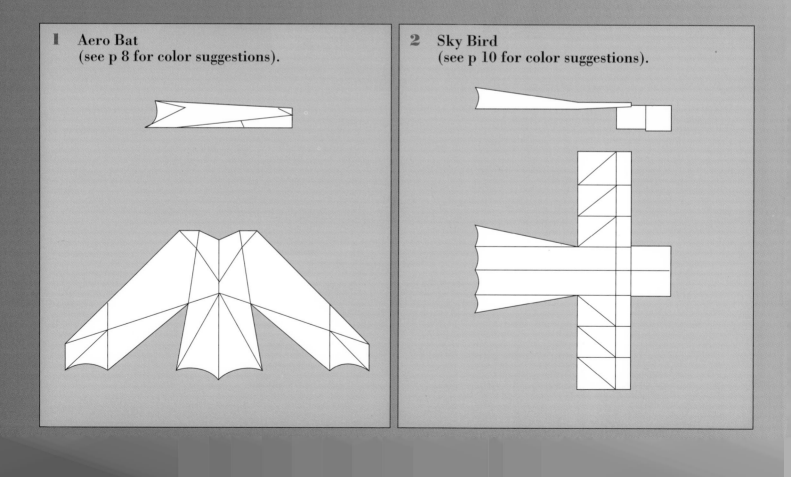

1 Aero Bat
(see p 8 for color suggestions).

2 Sky Bird
(see p 10 for color suggestions).

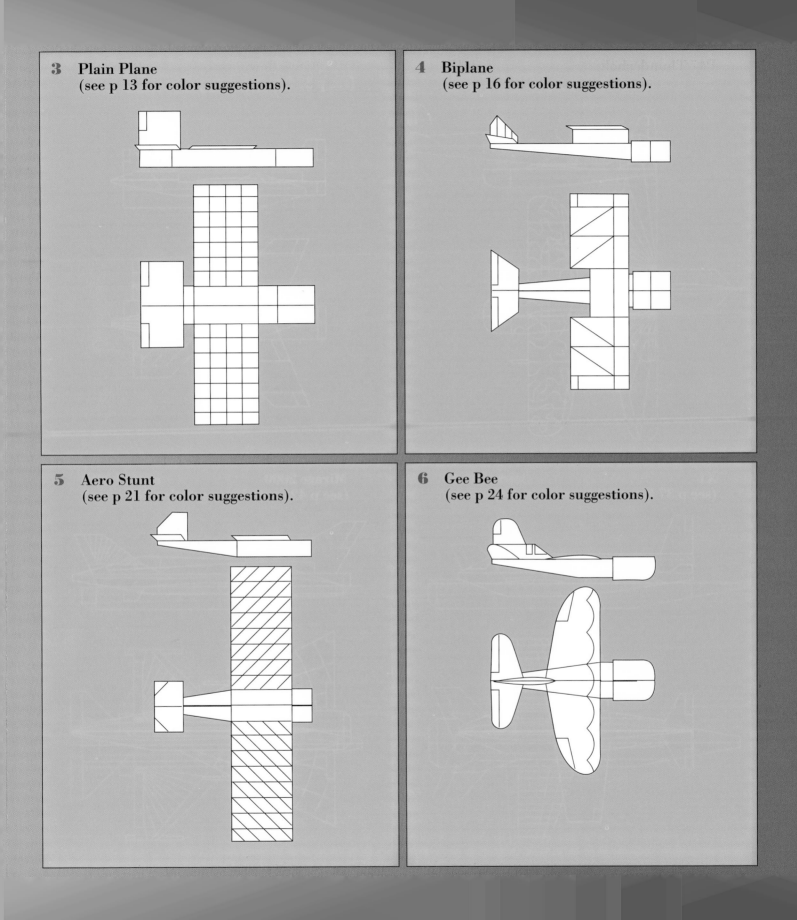

3 Plain Plane
(see p 13 for color suggestions).

4 Biplane
(see p 16 for color suggestions).

5 Aero Stunt
(see p 21 for color suggestions).

6 Gee Bee
(see p 24 for color suggestions).

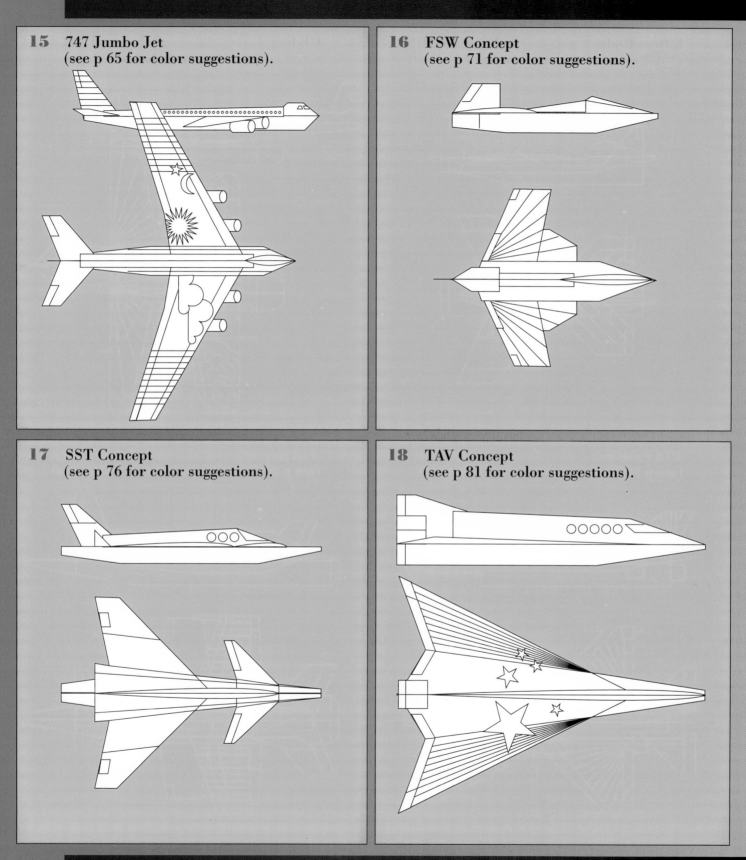

15 747 Jumbo Jet
(see p 65 for color suggestions).

16 FSW Concept
(see p 71 for color suggestions).

17 SST Concept
(see p 76 for color suggestions).

18 TAV Concept
(see p 81 for color suggestions).

Glossary

Angle of attack The downward slant, from front to back, of a wing.

Angle of bank The raising of the outside wing and lowering of the inside wing during a turn.

Aspect ratio The length of a wing in relation to its width. The longer a wing, the higher its aspect ratio.

Attitude The direction an airplane is pointing in relation to the horizon (banking, yawing, or pitching).

Ballast Extra weight needed in the nose of an airplane to make the center of gravity coincide with the wings, which provide the lift.

Control surfaces Small surfaces that can be bent to alter the airflow and change an airplane's attitude — ailerons for bank, elevators for pitch, and rudders for yaw.

Dihedral angle Upward slanting of wings away from the fuselage. (Downward slanting is called anhedral.)

Drag The resistance of air on moving objects, slowing them down.

Fuselage The body of an airplane.

Leading edges The front edges of wings, tails, or other parts.

Lift The force of air pressure beneath the wings buoying up an airplane.

Maneuver Skilfully making an airplane fly in a desired direction — turn, climb, dive, stall, spin, or loop.

Pitch Nose up or nose down attitude.

Roll Rotation along the length of an airplane.

Spar The main internal frame that supports the wing.

Strakes Wedge-shaped extensions of the wing's leading (front) edges near the fuselage.

Trailing edges The back edges of wings, tails, or other parts.

Trim Making small adjustments to the control surfaces to affect the attitude of an airplane.

Trim drag The drag (resistance) produced from bending control surfaces into the airflow.

Ventral fin A small stabilizer on each side of the fuselage underneath the tail.

Wing loading The amount of weight a given area of wing is required to lift.

Yaw Nose left or nose right attitude.

Flying Tips

Don't be discouraged if on first flight your paper airplane "corkscrews" and crashes. Flying paper airplanes is a delicate balancing act. Only when everything works in harmony – wings, horizontal tail, vertical tail, and control surfaces – is successful flight achieved. With each paper airplane that you build, aim to improve the construction. When carefully made and trimmed, the paper airplanes in this book are super flyers. But remember, the performance of each airplane differs. Experimentation is necessary in order to achieve maximum performance. This is part of the fun of flying paper planes.

Folds that are not neat and crisp add drag to the airplane. This will decrease glide performance. Sloppy folds can also result in twisted airplanes. Inaccurate gluing does not help matters. A twisted plane is sure to "corkscrew" badly (see p 7). The importance of careful folds cannot be over emphasized.

Airplanes must be symmetrical – one side must be just like the other. On both sides wing and horizontal tail sizes, shapes, and thicknesses must be the same. Also make sure that the control surfaces on one side are the same sizes and are bent the same amount as on the other side.

Make sure that the dihedral (upward slanting of wings and tail) is adjusted correctly. In each design, refer to the last step of construction for suggestions. Sometimes experimentation with different dihedral (or none at all) will be successful. Dihedral povides stability, however, too much dihedral has a destabilizing effect.

Some of the airplanes in this book have secondary control surfaces(flaps). Secondary control surfaces need special mention. If they are bent down slightly, lift is increased. If they are bent down 90° drag is greatly increased and the nose will pitch down. Additional up elevator is needed, increasing the angle of attack but also increasing drag. Trimmed in this way an airplane does not glide very far. In full-sized airplanes, this trim is good for landing. Experiment with different settings of the secondary control surfaces. Adjust carefully for best results.

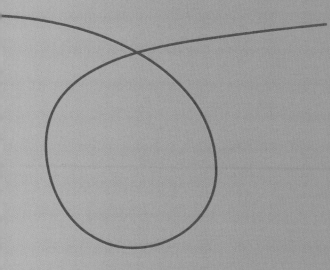

Paper airplanes are not baseballs. They cannot be thrown hard. To launch, hold the fuselage lightly between thumb and forefinger near the point where the plane balances. Throw with a firm forward motion keeping the nose level, pushing the airplane more than throwing it. With a bit of practice you will discover just how hard each of the planes need to be thrown under different conditions.

Pitch trim Although the paper airplanes in this book are built to resemble powered aircraft, they are obviously all gliders. For thrust they must convert altitude into airspeed (see p 10). The pitching axis is very important in determining airspeed. Once properly trimmed, an airplane will always fly at the same speed. If the airplane zooms toward the ground, bend the elevators up slightly to raise the nose. If more speed is needed, as in outdoor flight, less up elevator will produce the desired result.

Roll trim Providing the wings are not twisted, the wings should remain more or less level in flight. If one wing drops, bend the aileron on that wing down slightly and up slightly on the other wing.

Yaw trim   If the plane still has a tendency to turn, bend the rudder slightly opposite to the direction of the turn.

For additional information about trimming see pages 13, 16, and 21.

Further Reading

Boyne, Walter. *The Leading Edge*. Stewart,
Tabori & Chang, New York, 1986.

Mackie, Dan. *Flight*. Hayes, Burlington, 1986.

Schmidt, Norman. *Discover Aerodynamics With Paper Airplanes*. Peguis, Winnipeg, 1991.

Schmidt, Norman. *Best Ever Paper Airplanes*. Sterling/Tamos, New York, 1994.

Taylor, Michael. *History of Flight*. Crescent, New York, 1990.

Index